Guilt-free BAKING

To Nanny, who taught me to feed; to those close to me, who like to be fed; and to those who inherited the ability to put on weight just by looking at food!

First published in the USA and Canada in 2015 by
Nourish, an imprint of
Watkins Media Limited
19 Cecil Court
London, WC2N 4EZ

enquiries@nourishbooks.com

Publisher: Grace Cheetham
Managing Editor: Rebecca Woods
Editor: Wendy Hobson
Art Direction & Design: Georgina Hewitt
Production: Uzma Taj
Commissioned photography: Matt Russell
Food Stylist: Gee Charman
Prop Stylist: Jo Harris
Americanizer: Beverly LeBlanc

ISBN: 978-1-84899-206-1

10 9 8 7 6 5 4 3 2 1

Typeset in Gotham
Color reproduction by PDQ, UK
Printed in China

Notes on the Recipes
Unless otherwise stated:
Use large eggs, and medium fruit and vegetables
Use fresh ingredients, including herbs
Recipes indicate the number of servings
Fat, saturated fat and calorie calculations are given
    for one serving
Spoons are level unless otherwise stated
1 tsp. = 5ml   1 tbsp. = 15ml   1 cup = 240ml

nourishbooks.com

Guilt-free BAKING

Low-calorie and low-fat sweet treats

Gee Charman

NOURISH
EAT WELL, LIVE WELL

Contents

Introduction

As a chef, low-fat, low-calorie cookbooks were always the ones I walked straight past in the bookstore. It's not because I don't want to eat healthily—like everybody else, I have to watch what I eat. But after trying a few of them, it seemed all the fun bits had been taken out. The food tasted like cardboard and had the texture of sawdust, and that seemed especially true of so many low-calorie and low-fat baking books.

I have inherited my mother's sweet tooth and I also just love to bake, so the option of having only one sweet treat a week—as many books suggest—is just never going to work for me, even though I am a firm believer in the 90-percent-good, 10-percent-bad rule when it comes to eating. So, when I was approached about writing a book, this seemed like the perfect one to start with. It means I can bake to my heart's content without risking an expanding waistline.

I have to admit, however, it has been a huge challenge. I didn't want to do what many cookbooks do and simply replace butter with margarine, make the portions the perfect size for a mouse or cut out all the sugar and fill the recipe with artificial sweeteners instead. You can do that without my help with any cake recipe in any book. But these alterations change the texture beyond all recognition, the results lack flavor and the cakes are full of chemicals.

Instead, I started to think about reducing the amount of butter without cutting it out altogether, and looked for other sources of moisture for the cakes. Fruit purees have been a revelation, because they add natural sweetness and moisture to sponge cakes. In a plain vanilla cake, for example, a lot of the flavor comes from the butter, so big, punchy flavor-boosters are also needed. Spices like star anise and cinnamon and herbs like lemon thyme fill the flavor void often created when you go low fat.

In traditional recipes, all sponges cakes have the same texture, but one of the bonuses in this book is that adding low-fat yogurt, grated apple or pureed pears means the texture of each cake

is different. Some are light and fluffy, others are rich and sticky—but they are all delicious.

My grandmother loved to bake for other people, and I think I have inherited that from her. While testing the recipes in this book, I could have five cakes on the go at once, so friends, family, neighbors and even my yoga class were often recipients of cake boxes full of sweet treats, which were gratefully received and scoffed by even the most avid of yogis!

Only on one occasion did my dad say, "this tastes low fat." But when I looked, he was eating a plain slab of sponge cake that was meant to be filled with yogurt and fresh fruit. After a little bit of structural engineering, where bites had been taken out of it, I managed to stack it up with all the "fluffy bits," as Dad would say. He tucked in and I was back on track ... "Oh yes, this taste good! And if this is low fat, I can eat more of it—right?" Well, no, Dad, but it's great that you are loving the cakes that much. I guess the moral of this story is that sometimes the individual elements of low-fat cakes might not work on their own, but adorned with the "fluffy bits," they look and taste great.

With a growing obesity problem in the developed world, cutting down on the fat and calories we eat can't be a bad thing. What I am trying to do is keep all the good bits and just remove some of the bad. Even low-fat, low-calorie cakes have to be eaten with a warning, however—just because the calories

are lower it doesn't mean you can eat ten! The benefit is that with the treats you do have, you can have them a little more often and they won't do you any harm, but they still have to be eaten as part of a healthy, balanced diet. I can't conjure up a way around that—sorry! But I have succeeded in including lots of oats, fruit and vegetables in these recipes, which is an added bonus in that they are both healthier and keep you fuller for longer. Plus they stop the sugar rush you get with traditional cakes—which are packed with sugar— making resisting a second helping a little easier.

Every recipe indicates the number of servings it makes, and each serving contains a maximum of 300 calories and 6g of fat—most a lot less. They also give you the preparation and baking times —since most of these treats are served cold, that doesn't include the cooling time. If, like me, you find cakes are difficult to resist once they have cooled and are safely in the cake tin, I have tried to help by adding storage advice. Because some of us will be tempted to nibble too often at a cake that will remain at its best for a few days, many of the cakes can be made, a portion enjoyed, then the rest frozen for another day.

Whether it is for family and friends or for a sneaky treat on the couch, baking should be a pleasure, and with my recipes it will be, because they are all low in fat and calories—this is guilt-free baking at its best. So, I wish you happy baking and—even more importantly—happy guilt-free eating.

gee x

Filling the Freezer & Refrigerator

Low-fat baking uses a lot of fruit, so my refrigerator is always filled with fresh berries. I also keep apples and pears in the refrigerator, but that's a personal choice, because I like them cold and crunchy.

Although butter doesn't feature heavily in low-fat, low-calorie baking, I always keep a pack in the refrigerator. I also have a large pot of low-fat yogurt and lightest cream cheese, ready and waiting to make my cake batters and frostings.

My freezer also is a treasure trove of goodies. Frozen berries are always in the freezer, as well as the refrigerator, ready for fruity bursts in cakes and other baked goods. I often make large batches of fruit purees and freeze them in ice cube trays before popping them out into a freezer bag. It means I have them ready to hand and one stage of the baking process is already prepared. And when bananas get a little overripe, I peel and chop them and freeze them on a baking tray, then pop them in a freezer bag once they are solid, so they are ready to make Instant Guilt-free Banana Ice Cream (see page 21).

Once you have been through a baking spell, clear a space in your freezer, because some recipes will quite happily sit in there for a few weeks or months, then at midnight when the sweet tooth craving hits, you don't need to reach for a chocolate bar, but you will have homemade treats ready and waiting.

Because the cakes are just so tempting, it is sometimes a good idea to cool the cakes, then cut them into portions and wrap and freeze what you are not likely to use straightaway—then you can't go for the "it's a shame to leave just one slice" excuse. To help you, each recipe indicates how best to store the cake. They are all delicious freshly baked, of course, but if you do keep them, store the cakes in an airtight container, in the refrigerator, if necessary, or wrap and keep them in the freezer.

Key to the symbols

 Best eaten fresh or within hours of assembling

 Store in an airtight container up to the time indicated

 Store in an airtight container in the refrigerator up to the time indicated

 Wrap and freeze up to the time indicated

Stocking the Cupboard

When it comes to baking, a well-stocked cupboard is your best friend. I have a designated cupboard in my kitchen that is bursting at the hinges.

The best thing about a packed cupboard is that you can have all your dried ingredients to hand without needing to go out shopping every time you get the urge to bake. Plus, filling your cupboard with spices, dried fruit and nuts means you can jazz up a plain sponge cake recipe at the drop of a hat.

One word of advice: after years of baking I have learned the value of plastic containers. Using them means that flour doesn't get everywhere as you try to close the bag, and the open bag of nuts doesn't empty itself all over the kitchen floor as you go to grab it from the cupboard. Do label containers, though (I should have shares in marker pens)—otherwise you'll find yourself opening several boxes before you find the one you want or, as I have done, using all-pupose flour when self-rising was required. Cakes don't look or taste quite the same when you make that mistake.

Here are a few cupboard must-haves.

Flours & dry ingredients
- Baking powder
- Baking soda
- Cocoa powder, unsweetened
- Cornstarch
- Flour, all-purpose
- Flour, self-rising
- Flour, white bread
- Flour. wholewheat
- Oats, rolled and Scotch
- Rapid rise yeast

Fruit & nuts
- Dried fruit, such as apricots, cranberries, dates, golden raisins, raisins, sour cherries, etc.
- Nuts, such as hazelnuts, pecans, salted peanuts and walnuts
- Shredded coconut

Sweeteners
- Agave syrup
- Brown sugar, soft light and dark
- Confectioners' sugar
- Golden syrup or light corn syrup
- Honey

Spices & other ingredients
- Dark chocolate, 70% cocoa solids
- Fat-free sweetened condensed milk
- Low-fat evaporated milk
- Marshmallows
- Spices, such as apple pie spice, cardamom pods, dried edible lavender, ground cinnamon, ground ginger, nutmeg, star anise
- Vanilla bean paste
- Vanilla extract (not essence or flavorings)
- White chocolate (just a little, mind you)

Basic Recipes
The guilt-free fundamentals

It is always good to have a few basic recipes up your sleeve. And, the methods offered here can be easily incorporated into your own best-loved recipes to make them healthier—a favorite tart, for example, can be improved by a low-fat, low-calorie pastry.

All the recipes in this book are perfect to be served on their own, but you might like to make up one of these basic recipes to complement the dish—French Apple Tart (see page 108) with Guilt-free Vanilla Ice Cream (see page 20), for example, or Apple & Plum Crumble (see page 123) with Guilt-free Vanilla Custard Sauce (see page 19).

But don't forget that basic doesn't mean boring—far from it. These are bedrock recipes you will use over and over again.

Berry Coulis

PER SERVING:
  FAT 1G (OF WHICH SATURATES 0G)
  CALORIES 111
PREPARATION TIME: 10 MINUTES
COOKING TIME: 5 MINUTES

Put the berries, sugar, vanilla and ⅔ cup water in a saucepan over low heat and warm through a few minutes until the berries start to burst and release their juices.

Transfer the mixture to a blender and whiz until smooth, then rub the sauce through a strainer, using a wooden spoon or ladle to help you, and discard the seeds. Serve warm or leave to cool.

Makes about 1¼ cups (6 servings)

4 cups berries, such as raspberries, strawberries, blueberries, blackberries or a mixture
scant ½ cup superfine sugar
1 teaspoon vanilla extract

 7 days 3 months

Apple Puree

PER RECIPE QUANTITY:
FAT 1G (OF WHICH SATURATES 0G)
CALORIES 498 (83 PER SERVING)
PREPARATION TIME: 10 MINUTES
COOKING TIME: 10 MINUTES

Put the apples, sugar and 7 tablespoons water in a saucepan over medium heat and bring to a boil. Turn the heat down to low, cover with a lid and simmer about 8 minutes until soft, adding a little more water if the apples become dry.

Drain off any excess water, then mash with a fork to get a chunky puree or blend with a hand-held blender for a smooth puree. Leave to cool.

Makes about 3 cups (6 servings)

6 dessert apples, peeled, cored and
    cut into ¾-inch dice
1 tablespoon sugar
1 teaspoon ground cinnamon (optional)

 5 days 3 months

Pear Puree

PER RECIPE QUANTITY:
FAT 0G
CALORIES 330 (55 PER SERVING)
PREPARATION TIME: 10 MINUTES
COOKING TIME: 10 MINUTES

Put the pears, sugar and 7 tablespoons water in a saucepan and bring to a boil. Turn the heat down to low, cover with a lid and simmer about 8 minutes until soft, adding a little more water if the pears become dry.

Drain off any excess water, then mash with a fork to get a chunky puree or blend with a hand-held blender for a smooth puree. Leave to cool.

Makes 2½ cups (6 servings)

6 pears, peeled, cored and cut into
    ¾-inch dice
1 tablespoon sugar

 5 days 3 months

Pavlova

PER SERVING:
  FAT 0G
  CALORIES 164
PREPARATION TIME: 15 MINUTES
BAKING TIME: 1½ HOURS, PLUS OVERNIGHT
  COOLING IN THE OVEN

Preheat the oven to 225°F and line a cookie sheet with parchment paper. In a clean bowl, beat the egg whites, using an electric mixer, until stiff peaks form. Gradually add the sugar and continue beating until thick and glossy. Fold in the cornstarch and vinegar.

Spoon the meringue onto the prepared cookie sheet and spread it out into a circle about 8 inches in diameter, creating a dip in the middle of the circle with the back of a spoon. Bake 1½ hours, then turn the oven off and leave the pavlova to cool completely overnight in the oven.

Makes an 8-inch pavlova (6 servings)

4 egg whites
1 cup superfine sugar
1 teaspoon cornstarch
1 teaspoon white wine vinegar

 14 days

Meringues

PER SERVING:
  FAT 0G
  CALORIES 59
PREPARATION TIME: 15 MINUTES
BAKING TIME: 1½ HOURS, PLUS OVERNIGHT
  COOLING IN THE OVEN

Preheat the oven to 225°F and line a cookie sheet with parchment paper. In a clean bowl, beat the egg whites, using an electric mixer, until stiff peaks form. Gradually add the sugar and continue beating until thick and glossy.

Spoon the meringue onto the prepared cookie sheet in 12 neat piles. Bake 1½ hours, then turn the oven off and leave the meringues to cool completely overnight in the oven.

Makes 12 meringues (12 servings)

3 egg whites
¾ cup superfine sugar

 14 days

Guilt-free Piecrust Dough

PER SERVING:
   FAT 2.5G (OF WHICH SATURATES 1.5G)
   CALORIES 85
PREPARATION TIME: 15 MINUTES

Put the flour in a large bowl and rub in the butter, using your fingertips, until the mixture resembles coarse bread crumbs. Stir in the sugar, then use a fork to mix in the ricotta and gently blend to a smooth dough, adding up to 1 tablespoon chilled water, if necessary, a drop at a time, to bind the ingredients together. Wrap in plastic wrap and chill at least 10 minutes until required. Bake as specified in your recipe.

Makes enough for a 9-inch tart (12 servings)

1⅔ cups all-purpose flour, plus extra
   for dusting
2 tablespoons butter, chilled
1 tablespoon sugar
4 tablespoons ricotta cheese

 2 days

Guilt-free Crème Pâtissière

PER SERVING:
   FAT 1.3G (OF WHICH SATURATES 0.5G)
   CALORIES 79
PREPARATION TIME: 5 MINUTES
COOKING TIME: 10 MINUTES

Warm the milk and vanilla extract in a saucepan over low heat. Mix together the eggs, sugar and cornstarch, then gradually whisk them into the warm milk. Pour the mixture into a clean pan over low heat. Stir continuously until the mixture starts to thicken. It will become lumpy because of the cornstarch, but stick with it and use a whisk and a bit of elbow grease to beat out any lumps. Once it starts to bubble, cook 30 seconds, then remove the pan from the heat and spoon the custard into a bowl. Cover the surface with plastic wrap and leave to one side to cool.

Makes about 1½ cups (6 servings)

1½ cups skim milk
1 teaspoon vanilla extract
2 eggs
2 tablespoons sugar
⅓ cup cornstarch

 2 to 3 days

Guilt-free Vanilla Custard Sauce

PER SERVING:
    FAT 2G (OF WHICH SATURATES 1G)
    CALORIES 90
PREPARATION TIME: 5 MINUTES
COOKING TIME: 10 MINUTES

Put the milk in a saucepan over low heat. Scrape the seeds from the vanilla bean into the milk and add the vanilla bean. Mix together the cornstarch, agave syrup and egg yolks, then gradually beat them into the warm milk until blended. Remove the vanilla bean. (When it is dry, you can put it in a container of sugar to make vanilla sugar.)

Pour the mixture into a clean saucepan over medium heat. Stir gently until the custard thickens, then remove the pan from the heat immediately and pour into a pitcher. Do not leave it in the pan, because the residual heat might cause it to curdle.

Makes about 2 cups (6 servings)

2 cups skim milk
1 vanilla bean, split in half lengthwise
1 tablespoon cornstarch
3 tablespoons agave syrup
3 egg yolks

 2 to 3 days

Guilt-free Vanilla Ice Cream

PER SERVING:
    FAT 3G (OF WHICH SATURATES 1G)
    CALORIES 146
PREPARATION TIME: 10 MINUTES, PLUS AT LEAST
    6 HOURS FREEZING
COOKING TIME: 10 MINUTES

Put the milk in a saucepan over low heat. Scrape the seeds from the vanilla bean into the milk and add the vanilla bean. Mix together the cornstarch, agave syrup and egg yolks, then gradually beat them into the warm milk until blended. Remove the vanilla bean. (When it is dry, you can put it in a container of sugar to make vanilla sugar.)

Pour the mixture into a clean pan over medium heat. Stir gently until the custard thickens, then remove from the heat immediately and pour into a pitcher. Cover the surface with plastic wrap to prevent it from forming a skin and leave to cool.

Pour the cool custard into an ice-cream machine and churn until frozen, then store in an airtight freezer container in the freezer until needed. Alternatively, pour into a freezer container and freeze 2 hours, then break up the ice crystals with a fork and freeze again at least 4 hours.

Remove the ice cream from the freezer 15 minutes before serving to allow it to soften slightly.

Makes about 2¾ cups (6 servings)

2½ cups skim milk
7 tablespoons fat-free sweetened condensed milk
1 vanilla bean, split in half lengthwise
1 tablespoon cornstarch
3 tablespoons agave syrup
3 egg yolks

 5 months

Instant Guilt-free Banana Ice Cream

PER SERVING:
FAT 0.2G (OF WHICH SATURATES 0.1G)
CALORIES 120
PREPARATION TIME: 5 MINUTES, PLUS
4 HOURS FREEZING
COOKING TIME: 10 MINUTES

Put the banana slices on a cookie sheet and pop into the freezer 4 hours. Once frozen solid, put them in a blender with the agave syrup and start to blend. Pour the buttermilk through the funnel in the top of the blender and continue blending until smooth, then just serve—it's instant ice cream.

Makes about 2¾ cups (6 servings)

5 bananas, cut into ½-inch slices
2 tablespoons agave syrup or honey
7 tablespoons buttermilk

Guilt-free Frozen Vanilla Yogurt

PER SERVING:
FAT 1G (OF WHICH SATURATES 1G)
CALORIES 148
PREPARATION TIME: 10 MINUTES, PLUS
6 HOURS FREEZING

Mix together the yogurt and condensed milk. Scrape the seeds from the vanilla bean into the mixture. (You can put the vanilla bean in a container of sugar to make vanilla sugar.) Pour into a freezer container, cover with a lid and freeze 2 hours.

Remove from the freezer and mix with a fork to break down the ice crystals. Put it back in the freezer and leave 4 hours longer, or until set.

Remove from the freezer about 15 minutes before serving to let it soften slightly.

Makes about 3 cups (12 servings)

2 cups plus 2 tablespoons low-fat plain yogurt
¾ cup plus 2 tablespoons fat-free condensed milk
1 vanilla bean, split in half lengthwise

 5 months

Cupcakes, Muffins & Small Cakes

Good things come in small packages

I can't say I always agree with that statement, because when it comes to cakes it is often a case of the more the better, I say. But the beauty of cupcakes and muffins is that they are in their own perfect packages and there is not any need to share, because everybody can have their own.

A few of the best-known bakeries in New York have made cupcakes very fashionable in recent years, whereas they had previously been seen as rather retro baked goods only the kids would make. Now they come in all shapes, sizes and colors, and can look like little works of art.

Traditionally, cupcakes are covered in a thick layer of buttercream frosting, but for those of us who only have to look at a cake for their top pants button to pop open, buttercream is a no-go area. Instead, you have to get inventive and use lighter options, but that can be an advantage. If I'm honest, the cupcakes in bakery windows, with gravity-defying peaks of frosting, are a little sickly even for my sweet tooth. So my options are all about a little more cake and a little less frosting.

By baking your own, not only are you saving on the calories and grams of fat, guaranteeing all natural ingredients and enjoying far superior flavors, but you'll also find a saving in your pocket. When foods become fashionable, they become expensive, so the money saved is an added bonus.

Victoria Sponge Cupcakes

PER SERVING:
    FAT 4G (OF WHICH SATURATES 1G)
    CALORIES 190
PREPARATION TIME: 30 MINUTES
BAKING TIME: 18 MINUTES

Simple, light and classic—these are so easy to make, but unfailingly delicious.

Heat the oven to 350°F and line a muffin pan with paper cases or lightly spray the sections of a 12-hole loose-bottomed mini cake pan with low-calorie cooking oil spray.

Mix the flour and baking powder together in a large bowl. Put the pears in a blender and blend to a puree. In a separate bowl, beat together the oil, sugar, eggs and vanilla extract, then add the pear puree and mix well. Add the wet ingredients to the dry ingredients and mix together well.

Spoon the batter into the prepared muffin pan, filling the sections three-quarters full. Bake 15 to 18 minutes until golden brown, well risen and a skewer inserted in the middle comes out clean. Transfer to a wire rack to cool.

Remove the paper cases, if necessary, and cut the cakes in half horizontally. If you like, reserve 6 strawberries for decoration, then hull and thinly slice the remainder. Spread a little of the jam over one half of each of the cut cupcakes, then top with a few strawberry slices. Replace the top of each cake and dust lightly with confectioners' sugar. Cut the reserved strawberries, if using, in half. Make 3 cuts in each half up to the stalk, but not going through it completely, then fan them out and put one on top of each cake to serve.

Makes 12 cupcakes (12 servings)

FOR THE CUPCAKES:
low-calorie cooking oil spray, for greasing (optional)
2 cups self-rising flour
2 teaspoons baking powder
5 ounces canned pears in natural juice, drained
3 tablespoons sunflower oil
¾ cup sugar
2 eggs
2 teaspoons vanilla extract

FOR THE STRAWBERRY FILLING:
1⅓ cups strawberries
6 tablespoons low-sugar strawberry jam
1 tablespoon confectioners' sugar, sifted

 2 days 3 months without filling

Lavender Cupcakes

PER SERVING:
    FAT 4G (OF WHICH SATURATES 0G)
    CALORIES 160
PREPARATION TIME: 30 MINUTES
BAKING TIME: 18 MINUTES

Lavender gives a delightful subtle fragrance to these little cakes. You will find edible lavender in the baking aisle in major grocery stores or online.

Heat the oven to 350°F and line a 12-hole muffin pan with paper cases.

Mix together the flour, baking powder, salt and baking soda in a large bowl. Grind the lavender to a fine powder in a mortar and pestle, then add to the flour mixture. In a separate bowl, beat together the sugar, yogurt, vanilla bean paste, milk and oil. Add the wet ingredients to the dry ingredients and mix together well.

Spoon the batter into the prepared muffin pan. Bake 15 to 18 minutes, or until a skewer inserted in the middle comes out clean. Transfer to a wire rack to cool.

To make the icing, mix together the confectioners' sugar and food coloring, if using, then gradually work in enough of the lemon juice to make a thick, but spreadable, paste. Spoon the icing onto the middle of each cake, then help it out to the edges using the back of a spoon. Decorate each cupcake with a sprig of lavender, if you like, then leave to set before serving.

Makes 12 cupcakes (12 servings)

FOR THE LAVENDER CUPCAKES:
1⅔ cups self-rising flour
1 teaspoon baking powder
½ teaspoon fine sea salt
½ teaspoon baking soda
2 teaspoons dried edible lavender
½ cup sugar
1 cup fat-free plain yogurt
2 tablespoons vanilla bean paste
4 tablespoons skim milk
3 tablespoons sunflower oil

FOR THE LEMON & LAVENDER ICING:
1 cup less 1 tablespoon confectioners' sugar, sifted
a drop of natural purple food coloring (optional)
2 to 3 tablespoons lemon juice
12 tiny dried lavender sprigs on the stems (optional)

 2 days   3 months without frosting

Coffee Butterfly Cakes

PER SERVING:
FAT 4.5G (OF WHICH SATURATES 0.7G)
CALORIES 173
PREPARATION TIME: 30 MINUTES
BAKING TIME: 18 MINUTES

Butterfly cakes make a nice alternative to their more trendy cousins, the cupcakes. They look beautiful and use less frosting than traditional cupcakes. For somebody who only started drinking coffee at the age of 28, it might seem odd that coffee-flavored cake has always been my firm favorite. A little bit of me was lost when my favorite store stopped making their coffee cake loaf when I was at school. In fact, that might be what forced me to become a chef and an enthusiastic baker.

Heat the oven to 350°F and line a 12-hole muffin pan with paper cases.

Mix together the flour and baking powder in a large bowl. Put the pears in a blender and blend to a puree. In a separate bowl, beat together the brown sugar, eggs, pear puree, oil and coffee, using an electric mixer, until light and fluffy. Add the wet ingredients to the dry ingredients and mix together until just combined.

Spoon the batter into the prepared muffin pan, filling the sections three-quarters full. Bake 15 to 18 minutes until well risen, golden brown and a skewer inserted in the middle comes out clean. Transfer to a wire rack to cool.

To make the topping, dissolve the coffee, if using, in 1 tablespoon boiling water, then leave it to cool to room temperature. Beat together the cream cheese and 1 tablespoon of the confectioners' sugar until soft, then beat in the coffee or coffee extract to taste until well blended. Cover and leave to chill in the refrigerator.

Makes 12 cupcakes (12 servings)

FOR THE COFFEE CAKES:
1¾ cups plus 1 tablespoon self-rising flour
2 teaspoons baking powder
1 can (15-oz.) pears in natural juice, drained
⅔ cup packed light soft brown sugar
2 eggs
3 tablespoons sunflower oil
2 tablespoons very strong, cold black coffee
    or 1 tablespoon coffee extract

FOR THE CREAM CHEESE TOPPING:
1 tablespoon instant coffee, or coffee extract
7 tablespoons light cream cheese
1½ tablespoons confectioners' sugar, sifted

 1 day   3 months without topping

Using a small, sharp knife, press the point into the top of the cake at a slight angle, then cut around to remove a shallow upside-down cone from the top of each cake. Remove these in one piece, then cut each cone in half and leave to one side. Spoon or pipe the topping into the hole on top of each cake, then push the two halves of the cone into the frosting at an angle so they look like butterfly wings. Lightly dust with the remaining confectioners' sugar, if you like, to serve.

Chocolate Cupcakes with Avocado Frosting

PER SERVING:
FAT 4.5G (OF WHICH SATURATES 0.8G)
CALORIES 111
PREPARATION TIME: 30 MINUTES
BAKING TIME: 12 MINUTES

You are going to have to trust me on this one. I know avocado seems an odd substitute for buttercream frosting, but it really works. It's smooth and creamy, and avocados naturally have such a delicate flavor, you quickly taste the chocolate over avocado. Of course, I know these are actually vegan cupcakes, but I just didn't want to use that word as it would put so many non-vegans off the recipe immediately. For once, you won't miss butter and eggs in this recipe. The cakes are truly moreish and amazingly moist. Try them once and you'll see.

Heat the oven to 350°F and line two 12-hole mini-muffin pans with paper cases.

Mix together the almond milk and vinegar in a large bowl and stir well, then leave to one side for a few minutes to curdle. Beat in the sugar, oil, vanilla extract and almond extract, if using, and beat until frothy. In a separate bowl, mix together the flour, cocoa powder, baking powder and baking soda. Add the wet ingredients to the dry ingredients and mix together well.

Spoon the batter into the prepared muffin pans, filling the sections three-quarters full. (Try spooning the batter into a pastry bag, cutting off the end and then piping it in.) Bake 10 to 12 minutes until a skewer inserted in the middle comes out clean. Transfer to a wire rack to cool.

To make the frosting, scoop the avocado flesh into a small blender or food processor. (Or use a bowl and work with a hand-held blender.) Add the cocoa powder and honey and process until smooth, then gradually add a little almond milk, a drop at a time, until the mixture just begins to hold its shape.

Makes 24 mini cupcakes (12 servings)

FOR THE CHOCOLATE CAKES:
1 cup plus 1 tablespoon almond milk, plus extra
    for the frosting
1 teaspoon cider vinegar
1 cup less 1 tablespoon sugar
3 tablespoons sunflower oil
1 teaspoon vanilla extract
½ teaspoon almond extract (optional)
2 cups self-rising flour
⅓ cup unsweetened cocoa powder, sifted
1 teaspoon baking powder
1 teaspoon baking soda

FOR THE AVOCADO FROSTING:
2 ripe avocados
4 tablespoons unsweetened cocoa powder, sifted
2 tablespoons honey
a little almond milk, to loosen

 2 days 3 months without filling

Spoon the frosting into a pastry bag fitted with a ½-inch star tip and pipe the frosting onto the middle of the cakes in a nice high peak. You do not need to cover the entire surface of the cake, because this will add too much frosting and, therefore, too many calories. Peel back the paper and enjoy—the great thing is they are so mini you can eat two!

Apple & Star Anise Cupcakes

PER SERVING:
    FAT 4G (OF WHICH SATURATES 1G)
    CALORIES 157
PREPARATION TIME: 30 MINUTES, PLUS
    AT LEAST 20 MINUTES INFUSING
BAKING TIME: 18 MINUTES

I think the range of spices available is underused in baking. Don't get me wrong, I love traditional cakes, but if you want something a little different, adding spices is an easy way to create new flavors while keeping the fat and calories low. In this recipe, the star anise balances out the sweetness of the apples and is a great way of spicing up the unusual topping. I promise you, you won't even miss buttercream frosting.

Put the milk and star anise in a small saucepan over low heat and bring to a simmer. Remove the pan from the heat, cover and leave to infuse about 20 minutes or—better still—overnight.

Heat the oven to 350°F and line a 12-hole muffin pan with paper cases.

Beat together the eggs, sugar and vanilla extract in a large bowl, using an electric mixer, about 5 minutes until light and creamy. Gradually pour in the oil, beating continuously, then discard the star anise from the milk and beat that in, too. Use a large metal spoon to gently fold in the flour and baking powder, then stir in the apple cubes.

Spoon the batter into the prepared muffin pan, filling the sections three-quarters full. Bake 15 minutes, or until golden brown and firm to the touch. Leave to cool in the pan 2 minutes, then transfer to a wire rack to cool completely.

Meanwhile, to make the topping, put the apples in a saucepan over medium heat with 1 tablespoon water, the sugar and 1 star anise. Bring to a boil, then turn the heat down to low, cover with a lid

Makes 12 cupcakes (12 servings)

FOR THE APPLE & STAR ANISE CAKES:
5 tablespoons skim milk
1 star anise
2 eggs
½ cup plus 2 tablespoons sugar
1 teaspoon vanilla extract
3 tablespoons sunflower oil
1 cup plus 3 tablespoons all-purpose flour
2 teaspoons baking powder
3 dessert apples, peeled, cored and cut into
    ½-inch cubes

FOR THE SWEET APPLE TOPPING:
1 baking apple, peeled, cored and finely diced
2 dessert apples, peeled, cored and
    finely diced
1 tablespoon sugar
13 star anise (12 optional)
1 teaspoon cornstarch or arrowroot

 2 days 3 months without topping

and simmer about 5 minutes until the baking apple has broken down and created a puree, while the dessert apple chunks stay whole. Mix the cornstarch to a paste with 1 tablespoon water, then stir it into the pan and cook 1 minute longer, stirring continuously. Remove the pan from the heat and leave to cool. Spread the apple mixture on top of the cupcakes and serve with a star anise on each one, if you like.

Strawberries & Cream Cupcakes

PER SERVING:
FAT 3G (OF WHICH SATURATES 1G)
CALORIES 136
PREPARATION TIME: 30 MINUTES
BAKING TIME: 10 MINUTES, PLUS 2 HOURS FOR
THE STRAWBERRY CHIPS

Strawberries and cream are a match made in heaven—but cream is usually a no-go area in low-fat recipes. So, here's a solution—use cream from an aerosol can. It is aerated, so it looks great and saves you beating, plus it is naturally lighter and you need less. The strawberry chips look and taste amazing, with the concentrated natural flavor.

Heat the oven to its lowest setting and line a cookie sheet with parchment paper. Spread the strawberry slices on the prepared cookie sheet and dust lightly with confectioners' sugar. Bake 2 hours, or until dark red and dry. Loosen from the paper while they are still pliable, then leave to cool and become crisp. Turn the oven up to 350°F and line two 12-hole mini muffin pans with paper cases.

To make the cakes, put the strawberries in a blender and blend until smooth, then pass the puree through a strainer, using a ladle to help you, and discard the seeds. Mix together the flour and baking powder in a large bowl. In a separate bowl, beat together the sugar, eggs, strawberry puree and oil, using an electric mixer, until light and fluffy. Add the wet ingredients to the dry ingredients and mix together until just combined.

Spoon the batter into the prepared muffin pans. Bake 8 to 10 minutes until well risen and a skewer inserted in the middle comes out clean. Transfer to a wire rack to cool.

Just before serving, squirt a little aerosol cream onto the top of each cupcake and finish with diced strawberries. Add a couple of strawberry chips to each cake, if you like.

Makes 24 mini cupcakes (12 servings)

FOR THE STRAWBERRY CHIPS (OPTIONAL):
12 strawberries, hulled and thinly sliced
2 teaspoons confectioners' sugar, sifted

FOR THE STRAWBERRY CUPCAKES:
1 cup strawberries, hulled
1⅓ cups plus 1 tablespoon self-rising flour
2 teaspoons baking powder
½ cup sugar
2 eggs
3 tablespoons sunflower oil

FOR THE STRAWBERRY CREAM TOPPING:
½ cup light aerosol real dairy cream
1 cup strawberries, hulled and finely diced

 3 months before assembling

Peach Melba Cupcakes

PER SERVING:
FAT 1G (OF WHICH SATURATES 0.7G)
CALORIES 148
PREPARATION TIME: 30 MINUTES
BAKING TIME: 15 MINUTES

These cupcakes are summer in a paper case. Full of sweet peaches and tangy raspberries, they are perfect for using up either the slightly hard or the overripe peaches in the bottom of the fruit bowl.

Heat the oven to 350°F and line a 12-hole muffin pan with paper cases or spray the sections of a 12-hole loose-bottomed mini cake pan with low-calorie cooking oil spray.

Beat together the eggs, sugar, yogurt and vanilla extract in a large bowl, then fold in the flour, baking powder and cinnamon. Finely dice the peaches and stir them into the batter.

Spoon the batter into the prepared muffin pan, filling the sections three-quarters full. Bake 12 to 15 minutes until a skewer inserted in the middle comes out clean. Transfer to a wire rack to cool.

To make the sauce, put the raspberries and confectioners' sugar in a blender and blend to a puree, then pass the mixture through a strainer, using a ladle to help you, and discard the seeds.

Remove the cakes from the paper cases. If you are serving them as a dessert with a fork, serve the sauce separately. Alternatively, spoon the sauce into a syringe (you can get one at your local drug store) or a pastry bag with a really fine tip and, from the side of each cake, pipe some of the sauce into the middle. (If you do it from the bottom, it runs out and looks messy from the top.)

Makes 12 cupcakes (12 servings)

FOR THE PEACH CUPCAKES:
low-calorie cooking oil spray (optional), for greasing
3 eggs
½ cup plus 2 tablespoons sugar
¾ cup plus 2 tablespoons fat-free plain yogurt
1 teaspoon vanilla extract
1¾ cups plus 1 tablespoon self-rising flour
2 teaspoons baking powder
1 teaspoon ground cinnamon
3 peaches, peeled and pitted

FOR THE RASPBERRY SAUCE:
1⅔ cups raspberries
1 tablespoon confectioners' sugar, sifted

 2 days ❄ 3 months without the sauce

Black Forest Cupcakes

PER SERVING:
FAT 6G (OF WHICH SATURATES 2G)
CALORIES 212
PREPARATION TIME: 45 MINUTES
BAKING TIME: 15 MINUTES

Here's a modern recipe inspired by a blast from the past. Black Forest gâteau was the signature dessert of the late 70s and early 80s, but it is now enjoying a revival—along with its companion, the shrimp cocktail. (For those too young to remember, the main course was steak and fries!) With my version, even those watching the calories don't need to resist this delicious treat (especially if you use water instead of kirsch).

Heat the oven to 350°F and line a 12-hole muffin pan with paper cases. Put the pears in a blender and blend to a puree.

Mix together the flour, baking powder and cocoa powder in a large bowl. In a separate bowl, beat together the brown sugar, eggs, pear puree and oil. Add the wet ingredients to the dry ingredients and mix until just combined.

Spoon the batter into the prepared muffin pan, filling the sections three-quarters full. Bake 12 to 15 minutes until risen and springy to the touch. Transfer to a wire rack to cool.

Meanwhile, to make the filling, put the cherries and kirsch in a small saucepan over low heat a few minutes until starting to soften. Remove the pan from the heat and leave to cool. Drain the cherries, reserving the liquid.

Use a small, pointed knife to cut out an upside down cone from the top of each cake, about ¾ inch in diameter. Remove these in one piece. Fill the holes with some of the cooked cherries, then cut off and discard the points of the cone and replace the tops on the cakes. Drizzle a little

Makes 12 cupcakes (12 servings)

FOR THE CHOCOLATE CUPCAKES:
5 ounces canned pears in natural juice, drained
1 cup plus 3 tablespoons self-rising flour
1 teaspoon baking powder
⅓ cup unsweetened cocoa powder, sifted
⅔ cup packed light soft brown sugar
2 eggs
3 tablespoons sunflower oil

FOR THE CHERRY FILLING:
1¼ cups dark red cherries, pitted and finely chopped
2 tablespoons kirsch or water

FOR THE CREAM CHEESE FROSTING:
7 tablespoons light cream cheese
1 tablespoon confectioners' sugar, sifted
½ vanilla bean, split in half lengthwise
12 cherries
1 ounce dark chocolate, 70% cocoa solids, grated

 2 days   3 months without filling or frosting

of the cherry cooking juices over the top so it soaks into the cakes..

To make the frosting, mix together the cream cheese and confectioners' sugar. Scrape the seeds from the vanilla bean into the mixture, then spoon it into a pastry bag fitted with a ⅝-inch star tip. Pipe a small blob of frosting just off middle on the top of each cake, then top with a cherry and a sprinkling of grated chocolate.

Marshmallow Cupcakes with Meringue Frosting

PER SERVING:
    FAT 2G (OF WHICH SATURATES 0G)
    CALORIES 220
PREPARATION TIME: 45 MINUTES
BAKING TIME: 15 MINUTES

This is a great recipe if you want to avoid butter-rich frosting, or when you just feel like a change. If you replace the milk with almond, soya or rice milk, then the cakes become a vegan-friendly offering—don't say I don't think of you! Just check the labels to make sure you are using totally vegetarian ingredients. You will need a candy thermometer for making these cupcakes. The frosting will develop a crust if you leave them for a day or so, but they will still be soft and gooey in the middle.

Heat the oven to 350°F and line a 12-hole muffin pan with paper cases.

Beat together the eggs, superfine sugar, milk, oil and vanilla extract in a large bowl. Mash the bananas with a fork, then mix them into the egg mixture. Sift the flour, cocoa powder, baking powder, baking soda and salt over, then add the marshmallows and fold all the ingredients together.

Spoon the batter into the prepared muffin pan, filling the sections three-quarters full. Bake 12 to 15 minutes until a skewer inserted in the middle comes out clean. Transfer the cupcakes to a wire rack to cool.

To make the frosting, put the egg whites, lemon juice, sugar and 2 tablespoons warm water in a large, heatproof bowl set over a pan of simmering water, making sure the bottom of the bowl does not touch the water. Beat, using an electric mixer, until the mixture reaches 158° to 167°F on a candy thermometer. Once you reach that temperature, remove the bowl from the heat and either transfer the mixture to a standard mixer or continue with

Makes 12 cupcakes (12 servings)

FOR THE MARSHMALLOW CUPCAKES:
2 eggs
½ cup plus 3 tablespoons superfine sugar
5 tablespoons skim milk
1 tablespoon sunflower oil
1 tablespoon vanilla extract
2 very ripe bananas
1¾ cups plus 1 tablespoon all-purpose flour
2 tablespoons unsweetened cocoa powder, sifted
1 tablespoon baking powder
1 teaspoon baking soda
¼ teaspoon fine sea salt
½ cup mini marshmallows

FOR THE MERINGUE FROSTING:
3 egg whites
1 teaspoon lemon juice
½ cup plus 3 tablespoons sugar
a few drops of food coloring (optional)
½ cup white mini marshmallows

 2 days   3 months without frosting

the hand-held mixer. You need to beat the eggs 12 to 15 minutes until stiff, glossy peaks form. Beat in a few drops of food coloring, if you like.

Spoon the frosting into a pastry bag fitted with a large star tip and pipe onto the cupcakes. Scatter with the remaining mini marshmallows to serve.

Go Fruity Muffins

PER SERVING:
FAT 5.6G (OF WHICH SATURATES 0.6G)
CALORIES 172
PREPARATION TIME: 15 MINUTES, PLUS
15 MINUTES SOAKING
BAKING TIME: 20 MINUTES

These are a perfect breakfast all-in-one treat—fruit, oats and apple juice in every mouthful. Remember not to overmix the batter when making muffins or they tend to become a little tough and rubbery. Keep it light in every way! The main difference between a cupcake and a muffin is that muffins are usually made with liquid fats, such as sunflower oil, and are not frosted, whereas cupcakes are made with butter and are usually topped with mounds of buttercream frosting. The fruit in these muffins can be changed to suit your own tastes and there is not any need to add a frosting.

Heat the oven to 350°F and line a 12-hole muffin pan with paper cases. Put the oats in a bowl, pour the apple juice over and leave to soak 15 minutes.

In a separate bowl, mix together the flour, baking powder and baking soda. In a third bowl, beat together the oil, sugar, eggs and vanilla extract, using an electric mixer, until light and creamy. Add the soaked oats and the egg mixture to the dry ingredients and mix together until just combined, taking care not to overmix, because this will make your muffins tough. Gently fold in the fruit.

Spoon the batter into the prepared muffin pan and sprinkle with the sunflower seeds. Bake 20 minutes, or until risen, golden brown and just firm to the touch. Transfer to a wire rack to cool.

Makes 12 muffins (12 servings)

¾ cup rolled oats
⅔ cup apple juice
1½ cups self-rising flour
1 teaspoon baking powder
1 teaspoon baking soda
3 tablespoons canola or sunflower oil
⅓ cup sugar
2 eggs
1 teaspoon vanilla extract
¾ cup raspberries
⅔ cup blueberries
1 dessert apple, peeled, cored and finely diced
1 tablespoon sunflower seeds

 4 days

Clementine & Cranberry Muffins

PER SERVING:
FAT 5G (OF WHICH SATURATES 3G)
CALORIES 171
PREPARATION TIME: 15 MINUTES
BAKING TIME: 20 MINUTES

With all the freshly grated clementine zest and the juice, your kitchen will smell like Christmas while these muffins are baking. If clementines or tangarines are not in season, just use one large orange instead so you can enjoy these treats all year around.

Heat the oven to 350°F and either line a 12-hole, deep muffin pan with paper cases or baking parchment, or place 12 mini nonstick loaf cases on a baking sheet.

Mix together the flour, baking powder and sugar in a large bowl. In a separate bowl, mix together the cranberries, clementine zest and juice, melted butter, eggs and yogurt. Stir the wet ingredients into the dry ingredients until just combined, taking care you do not overmix, because this will make your muffins tough.

Spoon the batter into the prepared muffin pan, filling each section three-quarters full. Bake 15 to 20 minutes, or until a skewer inserted in the middle comes out clean. Transfer to a wire rack to cool, then dust with a very light sprinkling of confectioners' sugar to serve.

Makes 12 large muffins (12 servings)

2 cups self-rising flour
2 teaspoons baking powder
½ cup sugar
½ cup ready-to-eat dried cranberries
grated zest and juice of 4 clementines or tangarines
3 tablespoons butter, melted
2 eggs
¾ cup plus 2 tablespoons low-fat plain yogurt
a little confectioners' sugar, sifted, for dusting

 4 days

Banana Bread Flowerpots

PER SERVING:
    FAT 1G (OF WHICH SATURATES 0G)
    CALORIES 300
PREPARATION TIME: 20 MINUTES, PLUS 3 HOURS
    RISING
BAKING TIME: 25 MINUTES

You are probably looking at this recipe and thinking, "I'm never going to make these—it's far too much trouble to go all the way to the nursery and spend $10 on flowerpots!" Well, if you are, you are a person after my own heart. I am a chef, but my heart does sink when I see a random piece of equipment or an ingredient that demands a separate journey to gather your wares before you can start messing up the kitchen and baking. But, I made this recipe for a big breakfast for a good friend's birthday, and the good old internet came up trumps, with mini flowerpots delivered to my door the next day. If yours is not a special occasion, however, you can easily shape the dough into rolls and pack them together on a baking sheet, or use a muffin pan—not quite as cute, but just as tasty.

Put the bananas and vanilla extract in a blender with 3 tablespoons of the honey and blend to a smooth puree. Tip into a measuring jug (unless your blender is calibrated) and top up with warm water so you have 1½ cups liquid.

Mix together the flour, yeast, salt and sugar in a large bowl, then make a well in the middle. Pour in the pureed bananas and start to mix together until you have a soft, but not sticky, dough. Turn the dough out onto a lightly floured countertop and knead about 10 minutes until the dough is smooth and elastic. Lightly oil a large bowl with low-calorie cooking oil spray. Put the dough in the bowl, cover with plastic wrap and leave to rise in a warm place 2 hours, or until it doubles in volume.

While the dough is rising, cut out 12 greaseproof paper circles the same diameter as the bottom of the flowerpots. Put a circle in the bottom of each

Makes 12 buns (12 servings)

3 large ripe bananas
2 teaspoons vanilla extract
⅓ cup honey
3½ cups white bread flour, plus extra for dusting
1 envelop (¼-oz.) rapid-rise dry yeast
1 teaspoon fine sea salt
2 teaspoons light soft brown sugar
low-calorie cooking oil spray, for greasing
12 mini terracotta flowerpots, about 2½ inches wide and 2 inches tall (new and unused in the garden, obviously)

 2 days

flowerpot, then grease the inside with low-calorie cooking oil spray. Do this two of three times to really "season" the pots, which will make it easier to turn out the bread when it is baked.

Turn the dough out onto a lightly floured countertop and knock the air out by punching it with your fist, then divide it into 12 equal pieces and roll them into fat sausage shapes. Put each sausage into a flowerpot. Bunch the pots closely together in a baking sheet, then cover lightly with parchment paper. Leave to rise 1 hour longer, or until double in volume and nicely filling the pots.

Meanwhile, heat the oven to 350°F. Bake 25 minutes until golden brown and hollow-sounding when you tap the tops. Turn the bread out and drizzle the remaining honey over. Serve warm as an amazing breakfast bread.

Iced Buns

PER SERVING:
    FAT 3.25G (OF WHICH SATURATES 1G)
    CALORIES 299
PREPARATION TIME: 20 MINUTES, PLUS 3 HOURS
    RISING
BAKING TIME: 15 MINUTES

Food—and especially baked goods—have always been a currency and a bargaining tool in our family. When my bottom was small enough to fit in the seat of a shopping cart, an iced bun was my reward for behaving well at the grocery store. After Mom had done her shopping, I would be wheeled over, in my food-filled chariot, to the bakery counter to choose which one I wanted ... which was always the biggest one!

Mix together the flour and salt in a large bowl, then rub in the butter, using your fingertips, until the mixture resembles fine bread crumbs. Stir in the sugar and yeast. Make a well in the middle of the flour and add the beaten egg followed by the milk and gently blend to a soft dough.

Turn the dough out onto a lightly floured countertop and knead 10 minutes, or until the dough is smooth and elastic. Lightly spray a clean bowl with a little low-calorie cooking oil spray. Put the dough in the bowl, cover with plastic wrap and leave to rise in a warm place 2 hours, or until it doubles in volume.

Line a cookie sheet with parchment paper. Turn the dough out again, knock the air out of the dough by punching it with your fist, then divide it into 12 equal pieces. Shape them into rope shapes and put them on the prepared baking tray, just touching. Cover the buns lightly with a piece of parchment paper and leave to rise in a warm place 40 minutes to 1 hour longer, or until they double in volume.

Heat the oven to 400°F. Remove the parchment paper cover and bake the buns 10 to 15 minutes

Makes 12 buns (12 servings)

FOR THE BUNS:
scant 4 cups white bread flour, plus extra for
    dusting
1 teaspoon fine sea salt
2 tablespoons butter
5 tablespoons sugar
1 envelop (¼-oz.) rapid rise yeast
1 egg, beaten
scant 1 cup skim milk
low-calorie cooking oil spray, for greasing

FOR THE ICING:
scant 2 cups confectioners' sugar, sifted
a few drops natural food coloring (optional)
3 tablespoons sugar strands

 2 days ❄ 3 months without frosting

until golden brown, risen and hollow-sounding when tapped on the bottom. Transfer to a wire rack to cool.

When the buns are cool, make the icing. Put the confectioners' sugar in a small bowl and gradually add 2 tablespoons water, a drop at a time, to make a stiff, but spreadable, paste. Add a few drops of natural food coloring, instead of some of the water, if you like. Dip the tops of the buns in the icing, then put on a wire rack set over a tray, dipped-side up. Sprinkle with sugar strands and leave to set before tucking in.

St. Clement's Drizzle Cakes

PER SERVING:
    FAT 4G (OF WHICH SATURATES 0.3G)
    CALORIES 155
PREPARATION TIME: 15 MINUTES
BAKING TIME: 20 MINUTES

Lemon drizzle cakes are fresh and tangy, and are perfect if you want a cake that lasts for a few days after baking. The sticky syrup you pour over the baked cake adds moisture, which is also helped by the zucchini in the batter. This is a twist on a plain lemon drizzle cake, with extra sweetness added by the orange zest and juice.

Heat the oven to 350°F and line 12 mini bread pans with parchment paper or mini bread pan liners.

Beat together the sugar, eggs and oil in a large bowl 3 minutes, using an electric mixer, until light and creamy, incorporating as much air as possible. Gently fold in the flour, baking soda and lemon and orange zests and mix well, then stir in the zucchini.

Spoon the batter into the prepared bread pans, Bake in the middle of the oven 15 to 20 minutes until well risen and just firm to the touch, or until a skewer inserted in the middle comes out clean. Cover with a clean dish towel and leave to cool in the pans 5 minutes, then transfer to a wire rack.

Meanwhile, to make the topping, put the lemon and orange juice and agave syrup in a small saucepan over low heat and bring to a boil, then simmer a few minutes until the liquid reduces by half and becomes slightly sticky. Slowly spoon the syrup over the warm cakes so it soaks into the sponge. Serve warm or at room temperature.

Makes 12 cakes (12 servings)

FOR THE LEMON & ORANGE CAKES:
¾ cup sugar
2 eggs
3 tablespoons sunflower oil
1⅔ cups self-rising flour
1 teaspoon baking soda
grated zest of 2 lemons
grated zest of 1 orange
1¼ cups grated zucchini

FOR THE LEMON & ORANGE SYRUP:
4 tablespoons lemon juice
juice of 1 orange
2 tablespoons agave syrup

 3 days ❄ 3 months

Pumpkin Puffs with Salted Pumpkin Seeds

PER SERVING:
   FAT 5.5G (OF WHICH SATURATES 0.8G)
   CALORIES 173
PREPARATION TIME: 30 MINUTES
BAKING TIME: 45 MINUTES

This cake was born out a mistake when writing another recipe for this book. I had run out of paper cases so thought I would bake the mixture in piles on a baking sheet just to see if the balance of spices was right. Like all good cooking mistakes —tarte tatin being my favorite example—a new recipe was formed, and here it stands, a perfect breakfast treat to enjoy with a morning cup of tea.

Heat the oven to 350°F and line a baking sheet with parchment paper.

Toss the diced pumpkin with the cinnamon, apple pie spice and 1 tablespoon of the oil, then tip into a baking dish. Roast 30 minutes, or until tender, then transfer to a food processor and blend until smooth. Cover and leave to cool to lukewarm.

Toast the pumpkin seeds in a dry skillet over low heat a few minutes just until they start to turn glossy, then sprinkle with the salt, toss together, then turn out onto a plate, crushing the mixture between your fingers.

Mix together the flour and baking powder in a large bowl. In a separate bowl, beat together the sugar, syrup, egg, the remaining oil and the cool pumpkin puree. Add the wet ingredients to the dry ingredients and mix together well.

Put 12 spoonfuls of the mixture onto the prepared baking sheet, leaving a 2-inch gap between each one. Sprinkle a few of the toasted pumpkin seeds over and bake 15 minutes until puffed and springy to the touch. Transfer to a wire rack to cool slightly, then serve warm or at room temperature.

Makes 12 puffs (12 servings)

2¼ cups diced peeled and seeded pumpkin
1 teaspoon ground cinnamon
1 teaspoon apple pie spice
4 tablespoons canola or sunflower oil
2 tablespoons pumpkin seeds
1 teaspoon fine sea salt
2 cups plus 1 tablespoon self-rising flour
1½ teaspoons baking powder
¼ cup plus 2 tablespoons packed light
   soft brown sugar
2 tablespoons golden syrup
1 egg

 2 days ❄ 3 months

Cookies

Ready, steady, dunk!

That was the traditional school game at lunchtime and for afternoon snacks. We used to sit with our cookie of choice and chosen hot drink, set the timer and get dunking. It was a bit like Russian roulette, as we wanted to hold on long enough to win, but not so long that our cookie broke off and sunk, wasted, to the bottom of the mug. I like to think that we were just taking science and math out of the classroom as, after years of practice, we decided that it all came down to cookie density, weight and angles—well, that was my excuse for devouring a whole package in one sitting.

The big problem with cookies is they are so easy to eat with every cup of tea or coffee from about 11 a.m. to 5 p.m. Because they are often small and unfilling, they easily disappear without us even thinking about the calories we are swallowing, so for my cookies, I decided the fewer the calories in each one the better.

Each recipe in this chapter makes 24 cookies, but because, as I said, I can never stop with one, I have made all the servings two cookies each, but each serving still falls below the 300 calories and 6g of fat limit. So, what are you waiting for? Get dunking.

Iced Lemon & Lavender Cookies

PER SERVING:
FAT 3.3G (OF WHICH SATURATES 2.1G)
CALORIES 130
PREPARATION TIME: 20 MINUTES, PLUS
    20 MINUTES CHILLING
BAKING TIME: 15 MINUTES

As a kid I used to make iced lemon cookies at the weekend when friends came to visit—it was Mom's way of keeping us all quiet. These are based on the recipe I used all those years ago, but with the sophisticated twist of the lavender.

Put the butter, syrup and lemon juice in a saucepan over low heat until the butter melts. Mix together the flour, baking powder, cream of tartare, sugar, lavender and lemon zest in a bowl. Pour the melted butter mixture over the dry ingredients and mix to a smooth dough, adding a drop of skim milk, if necessary. Roll the dough into a ball, flatten slightly, wrap in plastic wrap and chill in the refrigerator up to 20 minutes.

Heat the oven to 350°F and line a large cookie sheet with parchment paper.

Turn the dough out onto a lightly floured work surface and roll out to ½ inch thick. Use a 2-inch round cookie cutter to cut out 24 cookies, rerolling any off-cuts. Put the cookies on the prepared cookie sheet and bake for 12 minutes, or until they start to turn golden brown and begin to become firm to the touch. Leave to cool on the cookie sheet 5 minutes, then transfer to a wire rack.

Meanwhile, put the confectioners' sugar in a small bowl and the lemon juice in a separate bowl. Gradually mix the juice into the confectioners' sugar, a drop at a time, to create a paste slightly thicker than heavy cream so it sticks to the cookies. Add a little food coloring, if you like. Drizzle the icing across the cookies and sprinkle with chopped lavender. Leave to set 10 minutes before serving.

Makes 24 cookies (12 servings)

FOR THE LEMON & LAVENDER COOKIES:
3 tablespoons butter
2 tablespoons golden syrup or light corn syrup
2 tablespoons lemon juice
1⅓ cups plus 1 tablespoon all-purpose flour,
    plus extra for dusting
½ teaspoon baking powder
½ teaspoon cream of tartare
5½ tablespoons sugar
1 teaspoon dried edible lavender
grated zest of 1 lemon
a drop of skim milk (optional)

FOR THE LEMON ICING:
½ cup less 1 tablespoon confectioners' sugar, sifted
2 teaspoons lemon juice
a few drops of lilac food coloring (optional)
a few lavender sprigs, chopped (optional)

 3 days

Lime Fingers

PER SERVING:
FAT 3.3G (OF WHICH SATURATES 2.1G)
CALORIES 130
PREPARATION TIME: 20 MINUTES, PLUS
20 MINUTES CHILLING
BAKING TIME: 15 MINUTES

We tend to use lemon in baking a lot, while limes seem to be reserved for G&Ts—perhaps because the taste of limes can turn a little bitter when baked, instead of giving that refreshing sharp flavor of the lemon. That's why lime is always added to curries at the end of cooking. These little limy fingers, however, are baked for such a short time the lime becomes fragrant, rather than bitter, and the tangy icing gives all the cookies an extra boost and a limy kick.

Put the butter, honey and lime juice in a small saucepan over low heat until the butter melts. Mix together the flour, baking powder, cream of tartare, sugar and lime zest in a bowl. Pour the melted butter mixture over the dry ingredients and mix together to make a smooth dough. Roll the dough into a ball and flatten it. Wrap in plastic wrap, then chill in the refrigerator up to 20 minutes.

Heat the oven to 350°F and line a baking sheet with parchment paper.

Turn the dough out onto a lightly floured work surface and roll out to ½ inch thick. Cut into 24 finger shapes about ¾ x 2 inches, rerolling any off-cuts. Put the cookies on the prepared baking sheet and bake 12 minutes, or until they start to turn golden brown and begin to become firm to the touch. Leave the cookies to cool on the tray 5 minutes, then carefully transfer to a wire rack to cool completely.

Meanwhile, make the icing. Put the confectioners' sugar in a small bowl. Squeeze 1 to 2 teaspoons lime juice into a separate bowl, then gradually mix it into

Makes 24 cookies (12 servings)

FOR THE LIME COOKIES:
3 tablespoons butter
2 tablespoons honey
2 tablespoons lime juice
1⅓ cups plus 1 tablespoon all-purpose flour,
    plus extra for dusting
½ teaspoon baking powder
½ teaspoon cream of tartare
5 tablespoons sugar
grated zest of 1 lime

FOR THE LIME ICING:
½ cup less 1 tablespoon confectioners' sugar, sifted
1 lime

 7 days

the confectioners' sugar, a drop at a time, to create a paste just slightly thicker than heavy cream so it sticks to the cookies. Dip one end of each cookie into the icing, then lay the cookies on a wire rack. Finally, use a fine grater to grate the lime zest over the icing, then leave to set.

Jaffa Cakes

PER SERVING:
    FAT 6G (OF WHICH SATURATES 2G)
    CALORIES 141
PREPARATION TIME: 1 HOUR, PLUS
    2 HOURS CHILLING
BAKING TIME: 18 MINUTES

"Full moon, half moon, total eclipse"—one of my favorite adverts that instantly bring Jaffa cakes to mind. In the old days, when my hips did not expand at the mere sight of an extra calorie, I could devor a whole package of Jaffa cakes, taking my time to nibble around the edge, pick off the chocolate with my teeth, eat the jelly and then the sponge—disgusting, I know, but it delayed having to clean my room!

Line a 12- x 8-inch jelly roll pan with plastic wrap. To make the orange gelatin, put the orange juice and agave syrup in a saucepan over low heat and bring to a simmer. Simmer 5 minutes, or until it reduces by one-third. Soak the gelatin in cold water a few minutes until soft. Squeeze out the excess water, then add the gelatin to the pan and stir until they dissolve. Pour into the jelly roll pan, cover with plastic wrap and chill in the refrigerator 2 hours, or until firm.

Heat the oven to 350°F and line a 13- x 9-inch cake pan with parchment paper. Put the sugar and eggs in a heatproof bowl set over a pan of simmering water. Beat 10 minutes, using an electric mixer, until light and fluffy and doubled in size. You should be able to drip a "W" shape from the whisks that remains on the surface 8 seconds.

Put the butter in a pan over low heat until it starts to bubble, then slowly drip it into the egg mixture, beating all the time. Fold in the flour, taking care not to overmix. Spoon the batter into the prepared pan, swirling the tray to spread it out thinly and evenly. Bake 8 to 10 minutes until golden brown and springy. Transfer to a wire rack to cool.

Makes 24 cakes (12 servings)

FOR THE ORANGE GELATIN:
1 cup plus 2 tablespoons smooth orange juice
2 tablespoons agave syrup or superfine sugar
2 sheets unflavored gelatin

FOR THE SPONGE CAKES:
⅓ cup sugar
3 eggs
2 tablespoons butter
1 cup all-purpose flour

FOR THE TOPPING:
2½ ounces dark chocolate, 70% cocoa solids
a little low-calorie cooking oil spray, for greasing

 3 days

Use a 2½-inch round cookie cutter to cut out 24 circles of the sponge cake and put them on a wire rack set over parchment paper. Wipe a 1½-inch round cookie cutter with a little oil to prevent it from sticking, then cut out 24 circles of set gelatin and put them on top of the cakes.

Put the chocolate in a large heatproof bowl and rest it over a pan of simmering water, making sure the bottom of the bowl does not touch the water. Heat, stirring occasionally, until the chocolate melts. Leave to cool slightly, then drizzle over the cakes. Leave them to set, then store in an airtight container in the refrigerator or a cool place.

Custard Drops

PER SERVING:
   FAT 3.5G (OF WHICH SATURATES 1.2G)
   CALORIES 99
PREPARATION TIME: 30 MINUTES
BAKING TIME: 15 MINUTES

This is my take on custard cream cookies, little cookies traditionally made with custard powder and sandwiched with a rich buttercream filling. The indent in the top of this version, however. means you can fill them with a thick vanilla custard sauce instead.

Heat the oven to 350°F and line two cookie sheets with parchment paper.

Put the flour in a large bowl, then rub in the butter, using your fingertips, until the mixture resembles coarse bread crumbs. Stir in the sugar and custard powder. Mix together the milk and vanilla bean paste, then pour three-quarters of the liquid into the flour mixture. Stir to mix to a ball of dough, adding the remaining milk if the mixture does not bind together.

With floured hands, divide the dough into 24 equal pieces and roll into balls. Put them on the prepared cookie sheets, leaving a small gap between each one, then use a floured thumb to press down in the middle of each ball to make a dent in the middle. Bake 15 minutes until golden and beginning to become firm to the touch, then transfer to a wire rack to cool.

Meanwhile, make the filling. Mix together the custard powder and sugar in a bowl and gradually work in 1 tablespoon of the milk to make a thick paste. Put the remaining milk and the vanilla bean paste in a small saucepan over low heat until lukewarm. Pour the warm milk over the custard powder paste, mixing all the time. Pour the mixture back into the pan and return to a low heat. Bring slowly to a boil, stirring all the time, then boil

Makes 24 cookies (12 servings)

FOR THE CUSTARD COOKIES:
¾ cup plus 1 tablespoon all-purpose flour
3 tablespoons butter
¼ cup sugar
½ cup custard powder
3 tablespoons skim milk
1 teaspoon vanilla bean paste

FOR THE CUSTARD CREAM:
2 tablespoons custard powder
1 tablespoon sugar
½ cup skim milk
1 teaspoon vanilla bean paste

 7 days

1 minute, still stirring. Pour into a bowl, cover the surface with plastic wrap, to prevent a skin from forming, then leave to cool and set.

Spoon the set custard into a pastry bag fitted with a small tip. Pipe the custard into the indents in the middle of each cookie.

Cranberry & Mixed Spice Digestives

PER SERVING:
FAT 4G (OF WHICH SATURATES 2G)
CALORIES 107
PREPARATION TIME: 15 MINUTES
BAKING TIME: 12 MINUTES

Digestive cookies have their crumbs in both camps, savory and sweet. They are perfect with a bit of cheese for a snack or for some dunking action in your tea or coffee. This recipe makes no exceptions—they are perfect both ways.

Heat the oven to 350°F and line a cookie sheet with parchment paper.

Mix together the flour, oats, spice and sugar in a bowl. Rub in the butter, using your fingertips, until the mixture resembles coarse bread crumbs, then stir in the baking soda and salt. Stir in the vinegar and cranberries, then finally stir in the milk and mix to a soft dough.

Roll the dough out on a lightly floured work surface until it is ¼ inch thick. Use a 2½-inch round cookie cutter to cut out 24 cookies. Put the cookies on the prepared cookie sheet and bake 10 to 12 minutes until lightly golden and firm. Leave to cool on the cookie sheet 2 minutes, then transfer to a wire rack to cool completely. Now you can get dunking!

Makes 24 cookies (12 servings)

1 cup less 1 tablespoon wholewheat flour,
    plus extra for dusting
1 cup medium Scotch oats
1 teaspoon apple pie spice
1 tablespoon light soft brown sugar
3 tablespoons cold butter, diced
½ teaspoon baking soda
a pinch fine sea salt
½ teaspoon malt vinegar
¼ cup dried cranberries, finely chopped
5 tablespoons skim milk

 / days

Gingersnaps

PER SERVING:
   FAT 3G (OF WHICH SATURATES 1G)
   CALORIES 109
PREPARATION TIME: 15 MINUTES
BAKING TIME: 18 MINUTES

The name says it all really—crunchy little cookies that add a touch of spice to after-school snacks.

Heat the oven to 350°F and line two cookie sheets with parchment paper.

Put the butter, syrup and sugar in a small saucepan over low heat until the butter melts. Mix together the flour and ground ginger in a large bowl. Add the wet ingredients to the dry ingredients and mix together well.

With damp hands, roll teaspoonfuls of the dough into balls, then put on the prepared cookie sheets, leaving a 2-inch gap between each one to let them spread. You should have 24 cookies. Press them down lightly, then sprinkle the chopped ginger over.

Bake 12 to 15 minutes until golden brown. Leave the gingersnaps to cool on the cookie sheets 2 minutes, then use a metal spatula to transfer to a wire rack to cool completely.

Makes 24 cookies (12 servings)

3 tablespoons butter
4 tablespoons golden syrup or light corn syrup
¼ cup packed dark soft brown sugar
1¼ cups plus 3 tablespoons self-rising flour
2 teaspoons ground ginger
1 ball preserved ginger, finely chopped

 10 days

Sour Cherry & Almond Cantuccini

PER SERVING:
    FAT 3.6G (OF WHICH SATURATES 0.5G)
    CALORIES 183
PREPARATION TIME: 10 MINUTES
BAKING TIME: 40 MINUTES

Cantuccini literally translates as "coffee bread," as Italians traditionally dip these twice-baked treats into their coffee, so the cookies soften beautifully as they soak up the liquid. You can easily change the nuts and dried fruit to suit your own taste. If you store them in an airtight container, you can enjoy them for weeks to come.

Heat the oven to 350°F and line two cookie sheets with parchment paper.

Mix together the flour, sugar and baking powder in a large bowl. Stir in the milk, almonds, sour cherries and eggs, then mix everything together well to form a soft dough.

Turn the dough out onto a lightly floured work surface and divide in half. Shape each piece into a thick rope 8 inches long and put on the prepared cookie sheets, then press the tops down lightly. Bake 30 minutes, then remove the cookie sheets from the oven.

Turn the oven down to 300°F.

Cut each piece into 12 cookies about ¾ inch thick, using a serrated knife. Put the cookies back on the cookie sheets, flat-side up, and bake 10 minutes longer to dry out completely. Transfer to a wire rack to cool.

Makes 24 cookies (12 servings)

2¼ cups all-purpose flour, plus extra for dusting
¾ cup sugar
1 teaspoon baking powder
1 tablespoon skim milk
⅓ cup whole blanched almonds,
    roughly chopped
½ cup ready-to-eat dried sour cherries
3 eggs, beaten

 3 weeks

Classic Soft Amaretti

PER SERVING:
FAT 6G (OF WHICH SATURATES 1G)
CALORIES 124
PREPARATION TIME: 10 MINUTES
BAKING TIME: 12 MINUTES

There are two types of amaretti: Saronno and Morbidi. Amaretti di Saronno are the hard, crunchy cookies that are perfect for crumbling over ice cream or trifles, but Amaretti di Morbidi are the soft, chewy ones made from a meringue base. Morbidi are my favorite and perfect served with a cup of strong coffee.

Heat the oven to 350°F and line two large cookie sheets with parchment paper.

In a clean bowl, beat the egg whites, using an electric mixer, until stiff peaks form. Gently fold in the sugar and ground almonds, then fold in the almond extract until the ingredients are just combined and you have a smooth paste—do not overmix.

Spoon about 24 teaspoonfuls of the mixture, each about the size of a small walnut, onto the prepared cookie sheets, leaving a 1-inch space between them to let them spread. Bake 10 to 12 minutes until golden brown.

Transfer the amaretti to a wire rack to cool. Dust the amaretti with a little confectioners' sugar, if you like, before serving.

Makes 24 cookies (12 servings)

a little butter, for greasing
2 egg whites
½ cup plus 2 tablespoons granulated sugar
1¼ cups very finely ground blanched almonds
½ teaspoon almond extract
a little confectioners' sugar, sifted (optional)

 3 weeks

Saffron Biscotti

PER SERVING:
    FAT 4G (OF WHICH SATURATES 0.5G)
    CALORIES 174
PREPARATION TIME: 10 MINUTES
BAKING TIME: 40 MINUTES

The name for these Italian-style cookies comes from the Latin word *biscoctus*, which means "twice baked." These twice-baked cookies were a staple of the legions of the Roman army, because they keep so well, making them perfect for baking in big batches and storing in airtight containers. Now that your history lesson is over—let's get baking.

Heat the oven to 350°F. Put the milk and saffron in a small bowl and leave to soak 5 minutes.

Mix together the flour, sugar and baking powder in a large bowl. Add the hazelnuts, eggs and the saffron strands and their soaking liquid, then mix everything together to form a dough.

Turn the dough out on a lightly floured work surface and divide in half. Shape each piece into a thick rope 8 inches long and put on two nonstick baking sheets, or two baking sheets lined with parchment paper, then press the tops down lightly. Bake 30 minutes, then remove the baking sheets from the oven.

Turn the oven down to 300°F.

Cut each piece into 12 cookies about ¾ inch thick, using a serrated knife. Put the biscotti back on the baking sheets, flat-side up, and bake 10 minutes longer so they dry out completely. Transfer to a wire rack to cool.

Makes 24 cookies (12 servings)

2 tablespoons skim milk
a pinch saffron strands
2¼ cups all-purpose flour, plus extra
    for dusting
¾ cup sugar
1 teaspoon baking powder
⅓ cup skinned whole hazelnuts
3 eggs, beaten

 3 weeks

Florentines

PER SERVING:
    FAT 5.2G (OF WHICH SATURATES 2.7G)
    CALORIES 133
PREPARATION TIME: 20 MINUTES
BAKING TIME: 15 MINUTES

These are a twist on a classic Florentine. I have cut down the quantity of slivered almonds and replaced them with oats, which are much lower in fat and calories. These are slightly chewier than normal, but I love the texture and the flavor—they are like butterscotch: oaty, almondy chews with bursts of fruit and a citrus tang.

Heat the oven to 325°F and line two cookie sheets with parchment paper. Put the butter, sugar and flour in saucepan over low heat a few minutes until the butter melts. Remove the pan from the heat and gradually add the crème fraîche, stirring continuously until blended. Add the slivered almonds, oats, candied peel, apricots and cherries and mix together well.

Put about 24 teaspoonfuls of the mixture on the prepared cookie sheets, leaving a 1½-inch space between the spoonfuls to let them spread. Bake 10 to 12 minutes until golden brown. Leave to cool on the cookie sheets 5 minutes, then transfer to a wire rack and carefully lift the rack onto a paper-covered cookie sheet.

Meanwhile, put the chocolate in a large heatproof bowl and rest it over a pan of simmering water, making sure the bottom of the bowl does not touch the water. Heat, stirring occasionally, until the chocolate melts. Use a spoon to drizzle the Florentines with the chocolate. (You'll catch any drips on the parchment paper.) Leave to cool and set before serving.

Makes 24 cookies (12 servings)

2 tablespoons butter
⅓ cup sugar
2 tablespoons all-purpose flour
3 tablespoons low-fat crème fraîche or sour cream
¼ cup slivered almonds
⅓ cup rolled oats
2 tablespoons candied peel
heaped ¼ cup ready-to-eat dried apricots, finely chopped
⅓ cup ready-to-eat dried cherries or cranberries, halved
1¾ ounces dark chocolate, 70% cocoa solids

 3 days 3 months

Pistachio & Lemon Thyme Kisses

PER SERVING:
FAT 4.6G (OF WHICH SATURATES 0.5G)
CALORIES 109
PREPARATION TIME: 10 MINUTES
BAKING TIME: 12 MINUTES

Lemon thyme is totally different from everyday thyme. It has a sweet note that is perfect for baking and it goes wonderfully with pistachios.

Heat the oven to 350°F and lightly grease a baking or cookie sheet or line them with parchment paper.

Put the pistachios in a blender and pulse to blend until finely ground. In a clean bowl, beat the egg whites, using an electric mixer, until stiff peaks form. Gradually add the granulated sugar, ground pistachios and lemon thyme and continue beating until you have a smooth paste—do not overmix.

Fit a pastry bag with a ¾-inch plain or star tip, then carefully spoon the paste into the bag. Be as light-handed as possible, because you do not want to knock out any air from the paste. Pipe the paste onto the prepared baking sheet, trying to get little points on the tops. (If you do not have a pastry bag, drop small spoonfuls of the mixture onto the baking sheet.) Bake 10 to 12 minutes until light golden. Transfer the cookies to a wire rack to cool, then lightly dust with confectioners' sugar to serve.

Makes 24 cookies (12 servings)

a little butter, for greasing (optional)
1 cup shelled pistachio nuts
2 egg whites
½ cup plus 2 tablespoons granulated sugar
1 teaspoon lemon thyme leaves
1 tablespoon confectioners' sugar, sifted, for dusting

 3 days

Jammy Dodgers

PER SERVING:
FAT 3.6G (OF WHICH SATURATES 2.2G)
CALORIES 122
PREPARATION TIME: 30 MINUTES, PLUS
20 MINUTES CHILLING
BAKING TIME: 12 MINUTES

I never really understood why some store-bought vesions of these crisp, jam-filled cookies have smiley faces stamped into them ... as if we need any encouragement to eat them! Be sure to organize a cookie sheet that fits into your freezer before making the dough.

Put the honey, milk and butter in a small saucepan over low heat until the butter melts. Mix together the flour, baking powder, cream of tartare and granulated sugar in a bowl. Pour the butter mixture over and mix everything together to form a soft dough. Roll the dough out on a piece of parchment paper until it is about ½ inch thick, then slide the paper onto a cookie sheet, cover with plastic wrap and chill 20 minutes.

Meanwhile, heat the oven to 350°F and line two cookie sheets with parchment paper.

Roll out the dough on a lightly floured work surface until ⅛ inch thick and use a 2¼-inch round cookie cutter to cut out 48 cookies. Put 24 of them on one cookie sheet. Use a 1-inch round cookie cutter or small heart- or star-shaped cookie cutter to cut out the middles of the remaining 24 cookies, then put these on the second cookie sheet. Bake 8 to 10 minutes until lightly brown. Transfer the cookies to a wire rack to cool.

Dust the 24 cookies with their middles cut out with confectioners' sugar. Put ½ teaspoon of the jam in the middle of the 24 whole cookies. then carefully position the dusted cookies on top of the cookies spread with jam. Press down lightly and serve.

Makes 24 cookies (12 servings)

3 tablespoons honey
2 tablespoons skim milk
3 tablespoons butter
1⅔ cups all-purpose flour, plus extra for dusting
½ teaspoon baking powder
½ teaspoon cream of tartare
5 tablespoons granulated sugar
1 tablespoon confectioners' sugar, sifted, for dusting
4 tablespoons low-sugar raspberry, apricot or black currant jam

 7 days 3 months for unbaked dough

Bourbon Cookies

PER SERVING:
    FAT 3.2G (OF WHICH SATURATES 1.8G)
    CALORIES 106
PREPARATION TIME: 25 MINUTES, PLUS
    10 MINUTES CHILLING
BAKING TIME: 10 MINUTES

To me, bourbon cookies scream the 90s. Not overly sweet, with a slight savory note of chocolate (I sound like a wine critic now!), they were—and still are—very moreish. These are my Oreo cookie when it comes to the ritual of eating them: top cookie off, bite off the cream, then devour the bottom cookie. I'm afraid it's not particularly ladylike, but it just has to be done!

Heat the oven to 315°F.

Beat together the butter and 3¼ tablespoons superfine sugar in a large bowl, using an electric mixer, until light and creamy, then beat in the milk. Stir in the flour, cornstarch, cocoa powder and baking powder and mix everything together really well until you have a stiff paste. Wrap the paste in plastic wrap and chill in the refrigerator 10 minutes.

Turn the paste out onto a lightly floured work surface and roll out until ⅛ inch thick, about the size that will fit on two nonstick cookie sheets. (This saves you from handling them too much.) Use a rectangular cookie cutter or a knife and a ruler to cut out 48 rectangles about ¾ x 1½ inches each, rerolling any off-cuts, if necessary, then put them on the prepared cookie sheets. If you like, you can decorate half the cookies with small indentations using the end of a skewer. Sprinkle with a tiny amount of superfine sugar, then bake 8 to 10 minutes until the cookies are just firm to the touch and dry, rather than shiny, on top. Carefully transfer them to a wire rack to cool.

Meanwhile, make the filling. Put the evaporated milk, coffee extract and cocoa powder in a saucepan over low heat a few minutes, stirring occasionally,

Makes 24 cookies (12 servings)

FOR THE CHOCOLATE COOKIES:
3 tablespoons butter, soft
3¾ tablespoons superfine sugar, plus 1 teaspoon extra for sprinkling
1 tablespoon skim milk
¾ cup plus 1 tablespoon all-purpose flour, plus extra for dusting
1 tablespoon cornstarch
3 tablespoons unsweetened cocoa powder, sifted
½ teaspoon baking powder

FOR THE CHOCOLATE FILLING:
2 tablespoons evaporated milk
1 tablespoon coffee extract
1 tablespoon unsweetened cocoa powder, sifted
⅔ cup confectioners' sugar, sifted

 7 days

until the cocoa dissolves and they are combined. Put the confectioners' sugar in a bowl and beat in the liquid until you have a thick paste, then leave to cool to room temperature.

Spoon the cool filling into a disposable pastry bag and snip off the tip. Take the undecorated cookies, which will be the bottoms, and squeeze a small line of the filling mixture down the middle of each one, taking care not to go right to the edges. Put a decorated cookie on top of each one and press down lightly to spread the filling, then leave to set.

Cocoa & Wholewheat Cookies

PER SERVING:
FAT 5.6G (OF WHICH SATURATES 3.2G)
CALORIES 157
PREPARATION TIME: 15 MINUTES
BAKING TIME: 12 MINUTES

I got this recipe idea from a semisweet cookie I picked up in Italy while shooting a TV show there. It's slightly sweet, very cocoa-y (if that's a word!) and nutty from the wholewheat flour. I appreciate wholewheat flour is mostly used to make bread, but it has that amazing fuller flavour that goes perfectly in these cookies.

Heat the oven to 350°F and line two cookie sheets with parchment paper.

Beat together the butter and sugar, using an electric mixer, until light and creamy, then beat in the vanilla extract and the eggs, one at a time. In a separate bowl, mix together the cocoa powder, flour, cornstarch, baking powder, baking soda and salt. Pour the wet ingredients into the dry ingredients and mix until you form a stiff dough. Add a little milk if the dough is too dry.

Put 24 teaspoonfuls of the dough, each about the size of a walnut, on the prepared cookie sheet, leaving a ¾-inch gap between each one. Bake 10 to 12 minutes until they are starting to firm around the edges. You want them still to be soft in the middle. Leave to cool on the cookie sheet 2 minutes, then carefully transfer to a wire rack to cool completely.

Makes 24 cookies (12 servings)

3 tablespoons butter, soft
⅓ cup packed light soft brown sugar
2 teaspoons vanilla extract
2 eggs
1 cup unsweetened cocoa powder
1⅔ cups wholewheat flour
1 tablespoon cornstarch
1 teaspoon baking powder
1 teaspoon baking soda
a pinch fine sea salt
a little milk (optional)

 6 days

Chocolate Chip & Raisin Cookies

PER SERVING:
FAT 4.1G (OF WHICH SATURATES 1G)
CALORIES 144
PREPARATION TIME: 15 MINUTES
BAKING TIME: 12 MINUTES

Cookies are very difficult to make without lots of butter, because it is the butter in the dough that gives them their texture. The inclusion of ricotta and oats, however, make these into chewy cookies with a little chocolate and fruit burst to top it off. The fruitiness of the raisins adds sweetness to the dark chocolate and the wholewheat flour means they actually fill you up, too.

Heat the oven to 315°F and line two cookie sheets with parchment paper.

Mix together the oats, cinnamon, both the flours and the baking powder in a bowl. In a separate bowl, beat together the oil, ricotta, sugar and eggs. Add the wet ingredients to the dry ingredients and mix together well. Stir in the chocolate chips and raisins, then mix again.

Put about 24 teaspoonfuls of the dough on the prepared cookie sheets, leaving a ¾-inch gap between each one. Bake 10 to 12 minutes until golden brown and firm to the touch. Leave the cookies to cool on the cookie sheets 2 minutes, then carefully transfer to a wire rack to cool completely.

Makes 24 cookies (12 servings)

½ cup rolled oats
1 teaspoon ground cinnamon
¾ cup plus 1 tablespoon wholewheat flour
⅓ cup plus 2 tablespoons all-purpose flour
1 teaspoon baking powder
2 tablespoons canola oil or melted coconut oil
3 tablespoons ricotta cheese
½ cup packed light soft brown sugar
2 eggs, beaten
heaped ⅓ cup dark chocolate chips
⅓ cup raisins

 2 days

Oat & Coconut Cookies

PER SERVING:
   FAT 6G (OF WHICH SATURATES 4.4G)
   CALORIES 275
PREPARATION TIME: 15 MINUTES
BAKING TIME: 18 MINUTES

Some cookies are meant to be hard and crunchy, but these little bites are soft and chewy; the coconut keeps them moist and makes them a sticky and delicious treat.

Heat the oven to 350°F and line two cookie sheets with parchment paper.

Put the butter, syrup and 3 tablespoons water in a small saucepan over low heat until the butter melts. Mix together the flour, coconut, oats, sugar and ginger in a large bowl. Pour in the melted butter and the milk and mix to a dough.

Turn the dough out onto a lightly floured work surface and roll into 24 balls. Put the dough balls on the prepared cookie sheets, leaving a ¾-inch gap between each one, and lightly press down to flatten them slightly. Bake 12 to 15 minutes until light golden brown. Leave the cookies to cool on the cookie sheets 2 minutes, then transfer to a wire rack to cool completely.

Makes 24 cookies (12 servings)

2 tablespoons butter
6 tablespoons golden syrup or light corn syrup
1 cup plus 3 tablespoons all-purpose flour,
   plus extra for dusting
½ cup shredded coconut
2¾ cups rolled oats
¾ cup sugar
1 teaspoon ground ginger
4 tablespoons skim milk

 6 days

Sheet Cakes, Bars & Brownies

Treats to share—whichever way you slice them

That is a motto I hold close to my heart. When I get stressed, I bake, and don't my friends and neighbors know it. For me, it often isn't even for the end result, it's more about the process. There is something about being distracted, measuring ingredients, using a bit of elbow grease for mixing and then the calming effect of the fabulous smells wafting from the oven. It's my form of therapy. Even if the end result wasn't important at the beginning, however, it soon becomes crucial once something delicious emerges from the oven.

Sheet cakes are great for pleasing a crowd. They are easy to make, and in one batch you have 24 cakes or bars ready to go. If you don't have a rectangular cake pan, you can always use the same size baking dish or roasting pan, lined with parchment paper.

Sheet cakes are so versatile as you can serve oaty ones for breakfast on the run for the whole family, top fruity ones with a spoonful of yogurt for dessert and enjoy all kinds for after-school treats or parties. The world is your oyster when it comes to flavor, so if, for example, you have blackberries in the refrigerator instead of blueberries, feel free to substitute to make a recipe your own.

Raspberry Battenburg-esque Cakes

PER SERVING:
   FAT 4G (OF WHICH SATURATES 1G)
   CALORIES 171
PREPARATION TIME: 20 MINUTES
BAKING TIME: 30 MINUTES

A family friend came to visit for Easter one year and brought a delicious, sticky almond cake. but when I politely asked for the recipe I was met with a stern, "no." It was her signature recipe and she would not give it up. I have to say, I was slightly cross, so I went into the kitchen and made my own version—and this is it. The best part of the story is that a few months later she asked for my recipe, because it was "so delicious." I, of course, graciously handed it over.

Heat the oven to 350°F and line a 12- x 8-inch cake pan or baking dish with parchment paper. Roll out the marzipan on a work surface lightly dusted with confectioners' sugar into a rectangle about 12 x 8 inches, then leave to one side.

Put the eggs, sugar, milk, oil and vanilla extract in a bowl and beat 5 minutes, using an electric mixer, or until light and creamy. Beat in the apple puree, then beat in the mashed bananas, using a fork. Add the flour, baking powder, baking soda and salt, then fold everything together.

Divide the batter in half. Stir the almond extract into one half and fold the raspberries and a few drops of pink food coloring into the other half. Spoon the raspberry batter into the prepared cake pan, then gently lay the sheet of marzipan on top, pressing down lightly. Spoon the almond batter on top and scatter with the slivered almonds. Bake 30 minutes, or until a skewer inserted in the middle comes out clean. Leave the cake to cool in the pan 30 minutes, then transfer to a wire rack to cool.

Warm the amaretto and agave syrup in a small saucepan, then brush over the top of the cool cake and leave to soak in. Cut into 24 squares to serve.

Makes a 12- x 8-inch cake (24 servings)

9 ounces store-bought golden marzipan
a little confectioners' sugar, sifted, for dusting
3 eggs
1½ cups sugar
⅔ cup skim milk
3 tablespoons sunflower oil
2 tablespoons vanilla extract
8 tablespoons Apple Puree (see page 15)
2 very ripe bananas, mashed
3⅔ cups all-purpose flour
1 tablespoon baking powder
2 teaspoons baking soda
1 teaspoon fine sea salt
1 teaspoon almond extract
a few drops pink food coloring
1⅔ cups raspberries
¼ cup slivered almonds
2 tablespoons amaretto
1 tablespoon agave syrup

 5 days 1 month

Lemon & Blueberry Drizzle Sheet Cake

PER SERVING:
FAT 2G (OF WHICH SATURATES 1G)
CALORIES 130
PREPARATION TIME: 25 MINUTES
BAKING TIME: 35 MINUTES

As the saying goes, "If it ain't broke, don't fix it." Well, when it comes to a classic lemon drizzle cake, the classic recipe certainly isn't broken. This version just has the addition of blueberries, which create extra little bursts of fruity flavor. The cake is really sticky and moist, so it is best eaten with a fork or you'll end up with very sticky fingers.

Heat the oven to 350°F and line a 12- x 8-inch cake pan or baking dish with parchment paper.

Beat together the butter and sugar in a large bowl, using an electric mixer, until light and creamy. Add the eggs, flour, baking powder, baking soda, lemon zest and yogurt and mix everything together well. Fold in the blueberries.

Spoon the batter into the prepared cake pan and smooth the top a little. Bake 30 to 35 minutes until a skewer inserted in the middle comes out clean.

Meanwhile, to make the drizzle mixture, warm the lemon juice in a small saucepan. Put the confectioners' sugar in a small bowl, add the lemon juice and mix well. Pour the mixture over the baked cake and leave to cool in the pan 5 minutes, then transfer to a wire rack to cool completely. Cut into 24 squares to serve.

Makes a 12- x 8-inch cake (24 servings)

FOR THE CAKE:
3 tablespoons butter
1 cup sugar
3 eggs
2¼ cups plus 2½ tablespoons self-rising flour
1 teaspoon baking powder
1 teaspoon baking soda
grated zest of 2 lemons
7 tablespoons fat-free plain yogurt
1 cup blueberries

FOR THE DRIZZLE:
juice of 2 lemons
1 cup less 2 tablespoons confectioners' sugar, sifted

 3 days

Fruity Oat Bars

PER SERVING:
FAT 6G (OF WHICH SATURATES 2G)
CALORIES 195
PREPARATION TIME: 15 MINUTES
BAKING TIME: 40 MINUTES

Some people like their oat bars crunchy, but I love them when they are super chewy—and these are just that. The little bursts of dried fruit scattered through the mixture bring them alive.

Heat the oven to 350°F and line a 12- x 8-inch cake pan or baking dish with parchment paper.

Put the bananas, melted butter, sugar, cinnamon and dates in a food processer and blend until smoother, adding a splash of water if the mixture is very thick. Reserve a handful of the cranberries and sunflower seeds, then mix the remainder with the oats, raisins and dried apricots in a large bowl. Pour in the banana mixture and mix well.

Spoon the mixture into the prepared cake pan and press down gently. Sprinkle the reserved cranberries and sunflower seeds over and press lightly again. Bake 35 to 40 minutes until golden brown. Leave the oat bars to cool 10 minutes, then cut into 24 squares while still warm and transfer to a wire rack to cool completely.

Makes a 12- x 8-inch cake (24 servings)

3 medium or 2 large bananas
3 tablespoons butter, melted
¼ cup packed dark soft brown sugar
2 teaspoons ground cinnamon
1¼ cups pitted dates, roughly chopped
scant 1 cup dried cranberries
1 cup sunflower seeds
heaped 4¼ cups rolled oats
⅔ cup raisins
scant 1 cup dried apricots, chopped

 7 days   3 months

Crunchy Granola Bars

PER SERVING:
  FAT 5.2G (OF WHICH SATURATES 2.4G)
  CALORIES 169
PREPARATION TIME: 15 MINUTES
BAKING TIME: 40 MINUTES

These bars require a little more effort than ordinary granola or cereal bar, because you have to toast the oats before making the actual bars, but the extra effort makes them really crunchy and perfect to give you plenty of energy on the go.

Heat the oven 350°F and line a 12- x 8-inch cake pan or baking dish with parchment paper.

Put the oats in a large bowl and stir in the butter. Spread the oats out on a baking sheet and bake 15 minutes, or until golden brown, stirring occasionally to prevent them from burning on the edge. Tip them onto a plate and leave to cool.

Turn the oven down to 325°F. Put the honey, apple juice and molasses in a saucepan over low heat a few minutes until warmed through and runny. Stir together the crunchy oats and rice cereal in a large bowl, then pour the warm honey mixture over and stir well to combine.

Spoon the mixture into the prepared cake pan and press down lightly. Bake 20 to 25 minutes until golden brown. Leave to cool in the pan about 15 minutes, then cut into 24 bars, using a sharp knife. Leave to cool completely before serving.

Makes a 12- x 8-inch cake (24 servings)

5½ cups rolled oats
7 tablespoons butter, melted
⅔ cup honey
½ cup apple juice
4 tablespoons molasses
1½ cups rice cereal

 7 days

Blackberry & Coconut Sheet Cake

PER SERVING:
FAT 5.9G (OF WHICH SATURATES 4G)
CALORIES 144
PREPARATION TIME: 20 MINUTES
BAKING TIME: 35 MINUTES

Like all berries, blackberries are best in season, otherwise they can be so sour they make your eyes water. If you want to make this cake when there are not any blackberries at the farm stands, pick up a bag of frozen berries and use those instead— you don't even have to thaw them first.

Heat the oven to 350°F and line a 12- x 8-inch cake pan or baking dish with parchment paper.

Mix together the flour, sugar and butter in a bowl, then scrape in the seeds from the vanilla bean. Rub in the butter, using your fingertips, until the mixture resembles coarse bread crumbs. Stir in half the oats and all the coconut. Reserve 6 large spoonfuls of the mixture and leave to one side. Add the eggs to the remaining mixture and mix until smooth, then add enough of the milk to make a thick batter.

Spoon the batter into the prepared pan and smooth the top a little. Scatter with the blackberries and sprinkle with the reserved crumb mixture, then scatter with the remaining oats.

Bake 30 to 35 minutes until golden brown and a skewer inserted in the middle comes out clean. Transfer to a wire rack to cool. Cut into 24 squares to serve.

Makes a 12- x 8-inch cake (24 servings)

2 cups self-rising flour
1 cup less 2 tablespoons packed light soft brown sugar
7 tablespoons butter
1 vanilla bean, split in half lengthwise
heaped 1 cup rolled oats
1¼ cups shredded coconut
2 eggs, beaten
7 tablespoons skim milk
2⅓ cups fresh or frozen blackberries

 3 days 1 month

Jamaican Ginger Cake

PER SERVING:
FAT 4G (OF WHICH SATURATES 2G)
CALORIES 141
PREPARATION TIME: 20 MINUTES
BAKING TIME: 30 MINUTES

There is a particular brand of store-bought Jamaican ginger cake my dad loves and his local store happens to stock it. Whenever my mom is away, a loaf seems to appear in the cupboard. I think he loves it because of its dense, sticky texture and lovely sticky top—and that's the result I achieved with this recipe. If you can leave this 24 hours before tucking in, it'll taste even better—it's a challenge, but worth the self-discipline.

Heat the oven to 350°F and line a 12- x 8-inch cake pan or baking dish with parchment paper.

Put the butter and sugar in a large bowl and beat together, using an electric mixer, until light and creamy. Beat in the syrup, then the eggs, one at a time, adding 1 tablespoon flour between each egg. Stir in the remaining flour with the baking soda, ginger, cinnamon and carrot and mix well, then stir in the milk.

Spoon the batter into the prepared cake pan and smooth the top a little, then scatter with the ginger. Bake 25 to 30 minutes until a skewer inserted in the middle comes out clean.

Leave the cake to cool in the pan. If you can resist, turn the cake out and store in an airtight container at least 24 hours before serving, because this makes the top become really sticky. Cut into 24 squares to serve.

Makes a 12- x 8-inch cake (24 servings)

7 tablespoons butter
½ cup packed dark soft brown sugar
generous ½ cup golden syrup or light corn syrup
2 eggs
3¼ cups all-purpose flour
2 teaspoons baking soda
1½ tablespoons ground ginger
2 teaspoons ground cinnamon
1 large carrot, grated
1 cup plus 2 tablespoons skim milk
4 balls preserved ginger, finely chopped

 4 days   3 months

Peanut & Jam Squares

PER SERVING:
FAT 5.8G (OF WHICH SATURATES 2.2G)
CALORIES 114
PREPARATION TIME: 15 MINUTES
BAKING TIME: 20 MINUTES

This is my take on a peanut butter and jelly sandwich. The old calories won't allow for loads of peanut butter, but I have managed to squeeze in a few salted peanuts to make up for it.

Heat the oven to 350°F and line a 12- x 8-inch cake pan or baking dish with parchment paper. Put the raspberries in a bowl and lightly mash with the back of a fork, then leave to one side.

Put the butter and honey in a saucepan over low heat and stir until the butter melts. Add the vanilla extract and stir in the oats. Spread half the mixture over the bottom of the prepared cake pan and press down firmly to level the surface. Spread with the jam and top with the mashed raspberries. Add the peanuts to the remaining oat mixture, then scatter this over the top of the raspberries.

Bake 15 to 18 minutes until golden brown. Leave to cool in the pan, then cut into 24 squares to serve.

Makes a 12- x 8-inch cake (24 servings)

2 cups raspberries
5 tablespoons butter
⅓ cup honey
1 teaspoon vanilla extract
heaped 3¾ cups rolled oats
3 tablespoons low-sugar raspberry jam
⅓ cup salted peanuts, roughly chopped

 6 days

Pumpkin & Cinnamon Blondies

PER SERVING:
  FAT 4G (OF WHICH SATURATES 2G)
  CALORIES 139
PREPARATION TIME: 15 MINUTES
BAKING TIME: 25 MINUTES

Blondies are white chocolate brownies, but because of the high fat content in white chocolate, my jeans just won't allow them in my diet. Instead, I use pumpkin puree, which you can easily buy, for that dense, squidgy texture we all love in brownies. It's low fat and perfect for baking.

Heat the oven to 350°F and line a 12- x 8-inch cake pan or baking dish with parchment paper.

Put the butter and sugar in a large bowl and beat together, using an electric mixer, until light and creamy. Beat in the eggs, one at a time, then stir in the pumpkin puree. Add the flour, cinnamon, baking powder and nutmeg and mix well.

Spoon the batter into the prepared cake pan and smooth the top a little. Bake 20 to 25 minutes until just set. Cover with a clean dish towel and leave to cool in the pan. Cut into 24 squares to serve.

Makes a 12- x 8-inch cake (24 servings)

7 tablespoons butter
1 cup plus 2 tablespoons dark soft brown sugar
2 eggs
1 cup pumpkin puree (pumpkin pie mix)
3¼ cups all-purpose flour
1 tablespoon ground cinnamon
2 teaspoons baking powder
1 teaspoon freshly grated nutmeg

 4 days ❄ 3 months

Chocolate & Beet Brownies

PER SERVING:
FAT 5.2G (OF WHICH SATURATES 1.9G)
CALORIES 129
PREPARATION TIME: 25 MINUTES
BAKING TIME: 25 MINUTES

I have never been a fan of beets and have always thought they taste like I imagine a worm would taste—earthy! Everybody has the right to change their mind, however, and I have now come to the conclusion beets are the best thing to use in low-fat brownies. There's not a hint of worm —just gorgeous, gooey chocolatiness.

Put the chocolate in a large heatproof bowl and rest it over a saucepan of simmering water, making sure the bottom of the bowl does not touch the water. Heat, stirring occasionally, until the chocolate melts, then remove the bowl from the heat and leave the chocolate to cool.

Heat the oven to 325°F and line a 12- x 8-inch cake pan or baking dish with parchment paper.

Put the eggs, vanilla extract, agave syrup and sugar in a bowl and beat, using an electric mixer, until light and creamy. Gently fold in the melted chocolate, then gently fold in the flour, baking soda and cocoa powder. Finally, stir in the beets, oil and milk. Spoon the batter into the prepared cake pan, smoothing the surface a little.

Bake 20 to 25 minutes until just set, but still slightly soft in the middle. Leave to cool in the pan 10 minutes, then transfer to a wire rack to cool completely. Cut into 24 squares to serve.

Makes a 12- x 8-inch cake (24 servings)

15 ounces dark chocolate, 70% cocoa solids
3 eggs
2 teaspoons vanilla extract
4 tablespoons agave syrup
1 cup less 2 tablespoons light soft brown sugar
1 cup plus 3 tablespoons self-rising flour
1 teaspoon baking soda
⅓ cup unsweetened cocoa powder, sifted
2½ cups peeled and finely grated beets
3 tablespoons sunflower oil
7 tablespoons skim milk

 5 days   3 months

Sticky Toffee Sheet Cake

PER SERVING:
FAT 6G (OF WHICH SATURATES 3.2G)
CALORIES 198
PREPARATION TIME: 30 MINUTES
BAKING TIME: 35 MINUTES

Sticky toffee pudding is my not-so-guilty pleasure. I remember cooking for a private dinner party hosted by a TV food critic and we spent the best part of 30 minutes arguing about what constitutes the perfect sticky toffee dessert. I went for dense, dark and sticky—so it almost sticks to the roof of your mouth —while he chose super-light and fluffy. I am doing it my way, because it's all a matter of taste and I think I'm right!

Heat the oven to 350°F and line a 12- x 8-inch cake pan or baking dish with parchment paper. Put the dates, vanilla, coffee extract and baking soda in a food processor and add 1½ cups boiling water. Blend together, taking extra care because of the steam from the boiling water, until you have a smooth puree.

Put the butter and sugar in a large bowl and beat together, using an electric mixer, until light and creamy. Beat in the eggs one at a time, then fold in the date puree and finally the flour.

Spoon the batter into the prepared cake pan and smooth the top a little. Bake 30 minutes, or until a skewer inserted in the middle comes out clean. Leave the cake to cool in the pan.

To make the sauce, put the condensed milk, brown sugar and butter in a saucepan over low heat and heat 3 to 4 minutes, stirring, until thick and dark. Leave to cool and thicken slightly, then pour over the cake and cut into 24 squares to serve.

Makes a 12- x 8-inch cake (24 servings)

2 cups pitted dates
2 teaspoons vanilla extract
4 tablespoons coffee extract
2 teaspoons baking soda
5 tablespoons butter, soft
1 cup sugar
4 eggs
3¼ cups self-rising flour

FOR THE SAUCE:
⅔ cup fat-free sweetened condensed milk
½ cup packed dark soft brown sugar
3 tablespoons butter

 5 days 2 months

Mocha Squares

PER SERVING:
FAT 6G (OF WHICH SATURATES 4G)
CALORIES 149
PREPARATION TIME: 30 MINUTES
BAKING TIME: 30 MINUTES

Although I have virtually given up drinking coffee, because I realized I was drinking far too much, I still love the flavor, so I haven't given it up all together. Now, one way I get my cappuccino hit is in cake form. It's a win-win in my book.

Heat the oven to 350°F and line a 12- x 8-inch cake pan or baking dish with parchment paper.

Put the butter, cocoa powder, brown and granulated sugars and coffee in a saucepan over medium heat and bring to a boil. Turn the heat down to low and simmer 1 minute, then remove the pan from the heat. Beat together the milk and eggs. Beat the flour, baking powder and baking soda into the melted butter and sugar mixture, followed by the egg and milk mixture.

Spoon the batter into the prepared cake pan and smooth the the top a little. Bake 20 to 25 minutes until a skewer inserted in the middle comes out clean. Turn the cake out of the pan and transfer to a wire rack to cool.

To make the frosting, mix together the cream cheese and confectioners' sugar. Spread over the cool cake, then dust with a little cocoa powder. Cut into 24 squares to serve.

Makes a 12- x 8-inch cake (24 servings)

7 tablespoons butter
½ cup unsweetened cocoa powder, sifted
½ cup packed dark soft brown sugar
½ cup granulated sugar
¾ cup plus 2 tablespoons strong coffee
7 tablespoons skim milk
2 eggs
2¾ cups self-rising flour
2 teaspoons baking powder
1 teaspoon baking soda

FOR THE MOCHA FROSTING:
¾ cup plus 2 tablespoons light cream cheese
1 cup less 2 tablespoons confectioners' sugar, sifted
1 tablespoon unsifted cocoa powder, sifted

 4 days 3 months without frosting

Arabian Honey Cake

PER SERVING:
FAT 6G (OF WHICH SATURATES 1G)
CALORIES 168
PREPARATION TIME: 25 MINUTES
BAKING TIME: 25 MINUTES

I lived in the Middle East for a while in 2009, and this cake was on every restaurant menu. It's traditionally made with rose water or orange blossom water, but if you are not a fan of either just replace it with a little more vanilla extract.

Heat the oven to 350°F and line a 12- x 8-inch cake pan or baking dish with parchment paper.

Beat together the sugar, eggs and oil for about 3 minutes, using an electric mixer, or until light and creamy to incorporate as much air as possible. Gently fold in the flour, baking soda, orange zest and juice and orange blossom water and mix well, then stir in the grated zucchini.

Spoon the cake batter into the prepared cake pan and smooth the top a little. Bake in the middle of the oven 20 to 25 minutes until risen and just firm to the touch, or until a skewer inserted in the middle comes out clean. Leave the cake to cool in the pan.

Meanwhile, to make the honey topping, warm the honey, orange juice, orange blossom water and cinnamon in a saucepan, then add the pistachios. Use a skewer to make a few holes in the cake before pouring the hot syrup over. Leave the cake to stand and absorb all the syrup while it cools. Cut into 24 squares to serve.

Makes a 12- x 8-inch cake (24 servings)

¾ cup sugar
4 eggs
6 tablespoons sunflower oil
3¼ cups self-rising flour
2 teaspoons baking soda
grated zest and juice of 1 orange
1 teaspoon orange blossom water
2½ cups grated zucchini

FOR THE HONEY TOPPING:
⅓ cup honey
juice of 1 orange
1 teaspoon orange blossom water
1 teaspoon ground cinnamon
½ cup shelled pistachio nuts, chopped

 3 days

Tarts & Pies

A sin-free way to lighten up your day

Well, it's not sin-free if you're talking about traditional tarts and pies. The battle over pastry has always been well fought among dieters. Pastry is full of fat and barely has an iota of goodness in it. The problem is that it tastes great and some of our best-known desserts and baked treats are surrounded by it.

Apple pie was a signature dish of my grandmother and her pastry was so short, it melted in your mouth. But when you watched her make it you could see why—butter, and lots of it. My solution is to use ricotta cheese instead in piecrust dough for pies and tarts, which reduces the fat and gives beautifully crisp results. The Guilt-free Piecrust Dough recipe (see page 18) can be adapted for savory dishes by leaving out the sugar, or, to jazz up sweet pies and tarts, why not add a little grated lemon or orange zest.

If you have a dinner party, pies and tarts are perfect to serve, because they can be made a day or two in advance and then stored in the refrigerator, But do watch out for any midnight refrigerator raiders ... you don't want to be a slice short.

Fig & Almond Tarts

PER SERVING:
  FAT 5.5G (OF WHICH SATURATES 2.6G)
  CALORIES 177
PREPARATION TIME: 25 MINUTES, PLUS
  10 MINUTES CHILLING
BAKING TIME: 20 MINUTES

I think raw figs are amazing, but warm figs are absolutely spectacular—they take on a whole new flavor and texture. They do need a little crunch to go with them, however, to balance out the softness and this is where their partner in crime comes into play—almonds.

Heat the oven to 375°F and line two cookie sheets with parchment paper.

Put the puff pastry dough on a lightly floured work surface and use a 3½-inch round pastry cutter to cut out 12 circles. Take a 2½-inch round pastry cutter and gently mark a border around each circle, making sure you don't cut all the way through. Put them on the prepared cookie sheets, cover with plastic wrap and chill in the refrigerator 10 minutes.

Carefully brush the outside ring with a little beaten egg yolk (reserving the rest for the ricotta mixture) and use a fork to prick the inner circle all over. Bake 10 minutes.

Meanwhile, put the ricotta in a bowl and stir in the lemon zest, 1 tablespoon of the honey and the remaining egg yolks. Mix everything together well. Remove the pastry circles from the oven and press the middle pieces down. Put 2 spoonfuls of the ricotta mixture into the middle of each circle. Cut a cross in the top of each fig, then put it in the middle of each circle. Bake 10 minutes longer.

Warm the remaining honey slightly to make it a little runnier, then drizzle it over the tarts and sprinkle with slivered almonds to serve.

Makes 12 tarts (12 servings)

1 sheet light puff pastry dough, about 14 x 10 inches
a little all-purpose flour, for dusting
2 egg yolks, beaten
⅔ cup ricotta cheese
grated zest of ½ lemon
4 tablespoons honey
12 just-ripe figs
1 tablespoon slivered almonds, toasted

Apricot & Rosemary Tart

PER SERVING:
FAT 4G (OF WHICH SATURATES 2G)
CALORIES 125
PREPARATION TIME: 30 MINUTES, PLUS
20 MINUTES INFUSING AND CHILLING
BAKING TIME: 20 MINUTES

My mom's amazing apricot tart started my love affair with *crème patissière* served with tart fruits, so I am particularly pleased with this low-calorie twist on our classic family recipe.

Heat the oven to 350°F. Put the milk and half the rosemary sprigs in a saucepan over low heat and scrape the seeds from the vanilla bean into the milk, then add the bean and heat until just lukewarm. Remove the pan from the heat and leave the milk to infuse 10 minutes. Discard the rosemary, then lift out, rinse and dry the vanilla bean. (You can put it in a container of sugar to make vanilla sugar.)

Mix together the eggs, egg yolks, sugar and cornstarch, then gradually beat in the warm milk. Pour the mixture back into a clean pan over low heat and cook 3 minutes, stirring continuously, until it starts to thicken. The cornstarch will become lumpy at first, but use a whisk and some elbow grease to get rid of any lumps. Once it starts to bubble, remove the pan from the heat and spoon into a bowl. Cover with plastic wrap on the surface of the custard and leave to cool.

Meanwhile, put the apricot halves in a baking dish, drizzle the honey over, then add the orange juice and remaining rosemary sprigs. Bake 10 minutes, or until they start to soften. Leave to cool.

While they are cooling, cut the phyllo dough sheets so they are 8 inches wide, keeping the sheets you are not using covered in a damp dish towel to prevent them from drying out. Brush the phyllo sheets with a little melted butter (they do not need to be completely brushed so concentrate

Makes a 14- x 5-inch tart (12 servings)

FOR THE CRÈME PÂTISSIÈRE:
1¼ cups skim milk
4 rosemary sprigs, plus extra needles for sprinkling
1 vanilla bean, split in half lengthwise
2 eggs
2 egg yolks
2 tablespoons sugar
¼ cup cornstarch

FOR THE APRICOTS, CRUST & TOPPING:
12 apricots, halved and pitted
1 tablespoon honey
juice of 1 orange or a little apple juice
4 sheets phyllo pastry dough, each 13½ x 12 inches
2 tablespoons butter, melted

around the edges), then line the bottom and sides of a 14- x 5- x 1¼-inch nonstick tart pan. You don't want any gaps, but it doesn't matter if you have to stagger them slightly. Push the dough carefully into the sides of the pan, then cover with plastic wrap and chill in the refrigerator 10 minutes. Bake 10 minutes, or until golden brown and baked through, then transfer to a wire rack to cool.

When all three elements are cool, spoon the custard into the pastry shell, top with the baked apricots, drizzle any roasting juices over and sprinkle with a few rosemary needles.

Cherry Bakewell Tart

PER SERVING:
FAT 4.4G (OF WHICH SATURATES 1.75G)
CALORIES 152
PREPARATION TIME: 25 MINUTES, PLUS
   10 MINUTES CHILLING
BAKING TIME: 50 MINUTES

I can hear people of Bakewell, in Derbyshire, England, shouting. I know it's not a classic Bakewell tart, but when you guys come up with such a great recipe, those of us watching the calories still want to enjoy it. This works equally well with raspberries, plum halves, blueberries or blackberries.

Heat the oven to 350°F and lightly grease an 8-inch deep, fluted nonstick tart pan with a little low-calorie cooking oil spray.

To make the dough, put the flour in a large bowl, then rub in the butter, using your fingertips, until it resembles coarse bread crumbs. Stir in the sugar, then use a fork to mix in the ricotta and gently blend into a smooth dough, adding up to 1 tablespoon water, if necessary, a drop at a time, to bind the ingredients together. Cover with plastic wrap and chill in the refrigerator 10 minutes.

Turn the dough out onto a lightly floured surface and roll out until ⅛ inch thick. Use to line the bottom and side of the prepared pan. Carefully push the dough into the flutes, leaving any overhanging dough attached. Line the dough with parchment paper and baking beans. Bake 12 minutes, then remove the paper and beans. Brush the bottom and side of the pastry with a little egg white, then bake 10 minutes longer, or until golden brown. Use a serrated knife to trim off any excess pastry.

Spread the jam over the bottom of the tart, then scatter the cherry halves over. Mix together the ground almonds, polenta, flour and superfine sugar. In a separate bowl, beat together the eggs, yogurt and almond extract. Add the wet ingredients to the dry ingredients and mix together well. Spoon evenly

Makes an 8-inch tart (12 servings)

FOR THE LOW-FAT PIECRUST DOUGH:
low-calorie cooking oil spray, for greasing
1 cup plus 3 tablespoons all-purpose flour,
   plus extra for dusting
2 tablespoons butter
1 tablespoon sugar
3 tablespoons ricotta cheese
1 egg white

FOR THE CHERRY FILLING & ALMOND TOPPING:
1 tablespoon cherry or raspberry jam
1½ cups pitted cherries, halved
¼ cup very finely ground blanched almonds
⅓ cup fine polenta or fine yellow cornmeal
2 tablespoons all-purpose flour
¼ cup sugar
2 eggs
⅔ cup fat-free plain yogurt
1 teaspoon almond extract
1 tablespoon confectioners' sugar, sifted

 2 days   1 month

over the cherries. Bake 20 minutes, or until just set with a slight wobble in the middle. Cool in the pan.

Meanwhile, put the confectioners' sugar in a small bowl and add about 1 teaspoon water, a drop at a time, stirring vigorously until you have a thick paste that just runs off a spoon. Drizzle in lines across the tart, then leave to set about 5 minutes before serving.

Plum & Cardamom Tart

PER SERVING:
    FAT 4G (OF WHICH SATURATES 2G)
    CALORIES 175
PREPARATION TIME: 40 MINUTES
BAKING TIME: 1 HOUR

By weight, cardamom is one of the world's most expensive spices and, like saffron, you need very little to make a big impact. If you take the seeds out of their papery cases, their flavor becomes super strong. You might know the flavor if you have ever bitten into a whole pod while eating a curry! In this recipe, the apple puree is infused with the whole pods to give the dish a subtle, warming flavor.

Heat the oven to 350°F and put a cookie sheet in the oven to heat, which will help the crust bake. Line a 10-inch loose-bottomed tart pan with parchment paper.

To make the dough, put the flour in a large bowl, then rub in the butter, using your fingertips, until the mixture resembles coarse bread crumbs. Use a fork to mix in the ricotta and gently blend to a smooth dough, adding enough of the iced water, a drop at a time, to bind the ingredients together. Cover with plastic wrap and chill in the refrigerator 10 minutes.

Meanwhile, put the apples, cardamom pods and 4 tablespoons water in a saucepan over low heat. Cover with a lid and bring to a boil, then simmer 5 to 10 minutes until the apples are soft. Discard the cardamom pods, then mash the apples to a puree.

Roll out the dough on a lightly floured work surface until it is ⅛ inch thick, then use it to line the prepared tart pan, leaving any overhanging dough. Line the pastry shell with a piece of parchment paper and cover with baking beans. Put it on the hot cookie sheet and bake 15 minutes, then remove the paper and baking beans and bake 5 minutes

Makes a 10-inch tart (12 servings)

FOR THE PIECRUST DOUGH:
1¾ cups all-purpose flour plus 1 tablespoon, plus extra for dusting
3 tablespoons butter
4 tablespoons ricotta cheese
7 tablespoons ice water

FOR THE PLUM FILLING:
3 large dessert apples, such as McIntosh, Jonathan or Gala, peeled, cored and cut into ¾-inch chunks
4 cardamom pods
1 pound 10 ounces ripe, but still firm plums, pitted and quartered
2 tablespoons smooth plum or apricot jam

 2 days

longer, or until just golden brown. Remove the pastry case from the oven and leave to cool slightly before using a serrated knife to trim off any excess pastry.

Spoon the apple puree into the bottom of the pastry case. Starting from the outside, fan the plum quarters around the tart, working your way into the middle. Bake 30 minutes, or until the plums are soft.

Transfer the tart to a wire rack to cool. While the tart is cooling, warm the jam in the microwave or in a small saucepan, then brush the top of the tart to give it a glaze. Serve cold.

Canterbury Tarts

PER SERVING:
FAT 6G (OF WHICH SATURATES 3G)
CALORIES 276
PREPARATION TIME: 40 MINUTES
BAKING TIME: 25 MINUTES

I first made a version of this tart when I was at cooking school and thought it was delicious and super easy to make. But the best thing about it is that at the same time it is both low fat and a total flavor explosion. All the flavors come from the naturally sweet fruits and not mountains of sugar and butter, and the filling is packed with juicy apple puree. It's a real treat and it feels like it. The phyllo pastry is a great way to cut the fat without banning pastry altogether, and a portion of my Guilt-free Frozen Vanilla Yogurt (see page 21)—or a good-quality store-bought one—is a perfect accompaniment to an apple tart. It is lower in calories and saturated fat than ice cream, although a serving with a Canterbury Tart would have to be a special occasion as it would push the calorie count over the 300 limit.

Heat the oven to 325°F and put a cookie sheet in the oven to heat, which will help bake the crust. Lightly spray six 3½-inch tartlet pans with low-calorie cooking oil spray.

Take 1 sheet of phyllo dough, keeping the sheets you are not using covered in a damp tea towel to prevent them from drying out. Brush it lightly with one-third of the melted butter, then sprinkle with one-third of the brown sugar. Top this with another 2 sheets of dough, brushing with butter and sugar as before, then top with the final sheet. Using a saucer or mug to guide you, cut out six 4-inch dough circles. Use the dough to line the prepared tartlet pans, gently pushing the dough into the flutes of the pans. Cover with plastic wrap and chill in the refrigerator while you make the filling.

Makes 6 tarts (6 servings)

low-calorie cooking oil spray, for greasing
4 sheets phyllo pastry dough, each 13 x 12½ inches
2 tablespoons butter, melted
4 tablespoons light soft brown sugar
3 eggs
½ cup plus 1 tablespoon sugar
3 tablespoons Apple Puree (see page 15)
grated zest and juice of 1½ lemons
6 dessert apples, cored

  1 month

To make the filling, mix together the eggs, sugar, apple puree, lemon zest and juice, then stir in the butter. Grate the unpeeled apples and stir them into the egg mixture, then spoon the mixture into the tartlet cases.

Pop the tarts onto the hot cookie sheet and bake 20 to 25 minutes until the middle of the tarts are just set and the pastry is a light golden brown. Transfer to a wire rack to cool slightly before serving warm.

French Apple Tart

PER SERVING:
FAT 2.2G (OF WHICH SATURATES 1G)
CALORIES 112
PREPARATION TIME: 25 MINUTES, PLUS
10 MINUTES CHILLING
BAKING TIME: 1 HOUR

This recipe is so simple to whip up when guests arrive unexpectedly. Literally five ingredients and you are away, and nobody will guess it is low in fat. Even the most novice of bakers can attempt this one and come out with a creation that not only looks beautiful, but also tastes great.

To make the apple puree, peel and core 2 of the apples then cut into ½-inch dice. Put them in a saucepan with 1 tablespoon water. Bring to a boil, then turn the heat down to low and simmer about 10 minutes until the apples start to break down into a puree, using a fork to help break up any big lumps. Puree with a hand-held blender, or in a blender if you like a very smooth puree. Tip the puree into a bowl and leave to cool. (If you want to miss out this step, you can easily use about 2 tablespoons applesauce.)

Heat the oven to 350°F and line a cookie sheet with parchment paper.

Give the sheet of puff pastry dough a couple of rolls on a lightly floured work surface to make it a little wider. Use a dinner plate about 10 inches in diameter as a guide and cut out a 10-inch circle of dough. Place the dough carefully on a nonstick cookie sheet. Crimp the dough by pressing the edge between the middle finger of one hand and the thumb and middle finger of the other hand to make a scalloped edge. Cover with plastic wrap and chill in the refrigerator 10 minutes.

Peel and core the remaining apples, then cut into slices about ⅛-inch thick. Remove the dough from the refrigerator and spread 2 tablespoons

Makes a 10-inch tart (12 servings)

5 crisp dessert apples, such as McIntosh
1 sheet light puff pastry, 14 x 10 inches (about 6 ounces)
a little all-purpose flour, for dusting
2 tablespoons honey
1 egg, beaten
low-fat crème fraîche or Guilt-free Frozen Vanilla Yogurt (see page 21), to serve (optional)

 2 days

of the apple puree over the bottom. Take the sliced apples and, starting from the outside of the tart and working inward, fan the slices out to cover the surface of the apple puree. Once the whole tart is covered (apart from the crimped edge), drizzle with the honey and brush the edge with a little beaten egg. Bake 30 minutes, or until the edge is golden brown. Serve warm with low-fat crème fraîche or frozen yogurt, if you like.

Jammy Tarts with Fresh Fruit

PER SERVING:
FAT 5G (OF WHICH SATURATES 2.3G)
CALORIES 175
PREPARATION TIME: 15 MINUTES
BAKING TIME: 10 MINUTES

I hated jam tarts as a kid. At every birthday party, a box would be produced and the brightly colored, sticky, sickly sweet, dry, crusted tarts would be handed around—horrid. Bad memories, however, can create great recipes, although these little jammy treats have only the vaguest resemblance to my childhood memory. You can use blueberries or pitted cherries instead of the raspberries, if you prefer, and any flavor of jam.

Heat the oven to 375°F.

Take the crustless slices of bread and use a rolling pin to roll them out until they are very thin. Brush one side of each slice with a little melted butter, then gently press each slice, butter-side down, into the molds of a 6-hole muffin pan. Push the bread right into the molds to create little baskets. Brush the insides with a little beaten egg. Bake 5 minutes, or until the bread is golden brown and crisp.

Put 1 teaspoonful of the jam in each bread basket, then put them back in the oven 5 minutes longer. Carefully transfer the baskets to a wire rack to cool.

When the baskets are cold, spoon in the yogurt, then top with the fresh fruit and serve immediately, with any leftover fruit served on the side.

Makes 6 tarts (6 servings)

6 thin slices white bread, crusts removed
2 tablespoons butter, melted
1 egg, beaten
6 teaspoons low-sugar jam of any flavor
6 tablespoons low-fat strawberry yogurt
2 kiwifruit, peeled and cut into ¼-inch half moons
1⅓ cups strawberries
1⅔ cups raspberries

Pear Tarts Tatin

PER SERVING:
FAT 6G (OF WHICH SATURATES 4G)
CALORIES 258
PREPARATION TIME: 30 MINUTES
BAKING TIME: 18 MINUTES

We all make mistakes in the kitchen, but sometimes those very disasters create legendary new dishes. Tarte Tatin was apparently such a dish, the result of two sisters dropping a single-crust apple pie on the floor, fruit-side up. Now however good this classic tart tastes, it is just too naughty for us, so my version combines all the best bits with a little less sin.

Peel the pears, leaving the stems attached. Cut a small slice off the bottom of each pear so they stand up. Use a melon baller to remove the core by scooping it out from the bottom of each pear. Stand the pears upright in a saucepan so they just fit in the pan. Pour in 4 cups water, then add the lemon zest and juice, cinnamon stick and 2 tablespoons of the sugar. Put the pan over high heat and bring to a boil, then turn the heat down to low and simmer 5 minutes, or until the pears are soft when pierced with the tip of a knife. Remove them from the heat and leave to cool.

Heat the oven to 400°F.

Cut 6 strips from the dough about 12 inches long and ½ inch wide. Brush the strips with a little beaten egg. Take a piece of dough and wrap one end around the top of the first pear, just at the bottom of the stem, and press the dough onto itself to seal and to secure it to the pear. Twist the dough around the pear in a spiral. When you get to the bottom of the pear, tuck the dough underneath, so the weight of the pear keeps it in place, then put the pear in a nonstick baking sheet. Repeat with the remaining pears. Bake 10 minutes, or until the pastry is golden.

Makes 6 tarts (6 servings)

6 just-ripe pears with stems
1 lemon, zest removed with a vegetable peeler, then juiced
1 cinnamon stick
5 tablespoons sugar
½ sheet (13-x 12-in.) rolled light puff pastry dough
1 egg, beaten
4 teaspoons butter
4 tablespoons sweetened condensed milk

Meanwhile, sprinkle the remaining sugar into the bottom of a nonstick skillet over medium heat for a few minutes until it caramelizes and turns golden brown. Remove the skillet from the heat and add the butter, stir to combine, then stir in the condensed milk and leave to cool slightly while the pears finish baking. Serve the pears hot with the caramel sauce.

Light Lemon Meringue Pies

PER SERVING:
FAT 3G (OF WHICH SATURATES 2G)
CALORIES 166
PREPARATION TIME: 30 MINUTES
BAKING TIME: 50 MINUTES

Sweet meringue and tangy lemon—these mini pies made in heaven, and you'll just love them.

Lightly spray a 12-hole mini muffin pan with low-calorie cooking oil spray.

To make the dough, put the flour in a large bowl and rub in the butter, using your fingertips, until the mixture resembles coarse bread crumbs. Stir in the sugar and lemon zest and then, using a fork, mix in the ricotta and gently blend to a smooth dough, adding up to 1 tablespoon water, if necessary, a drop at a time, to bind the ingredients together.

Roll out the dough on a lightly floured work surface until ⅛ in thick, then cut out twelve 2½-inch circles. Gently press the dough circles into the prepared pan, then brush with egg white, cover with plastic wrap and chill in the refrigerator 10 minutes while you make the filling.

Make the filling by beating together the superfine sugar, cornstarch and salt in a saucepan, then gradually whisk in 1¼ cups water. Bring to a boil, stirring, then turn the heat down to low and simmer 1 minute.

Beat together the lemon juice, zest and eggs in a bowl, then stir in a small amount of the hot water mixture. Beat this back into the water and sugar mixture. (This prevents the eggs from splitting.) Return the pan to the heat 30 seconds, then beat in the butter. Pour this into a bowl, cover the surface with plastic wrap and leave to cool.

Heat the oven to 400°F. In a clean bowl, beat the egg whites, using an electric mixer, until stiff peaks

Makes 12 pies (12 servings)

FOR THE PIECRUST DOUGH:
low-calorie cooking oil spray, for greasing
1 cup plus 3 tablespoons all-purpose flour, plus extra for dusting
2 tablespoons butter
1 tablespoon sugar
grated zest of 1 lemon
3 tablespoons ricotta cheese

FOR THE LEMON FILLING:
½ cup plus 3 tablespoons superfine sugar
⅓ cup cornstarch
1 teaspoon salt
½ cup lemon juice
grated zest of 2 lemons
2 eggs
2 teaspoons butter

FOR THE MERINGUE:
3 egg whites
3¾ tablespoons superfine sugar
¼ teaspoon cream of tartare

 3 days

form. Gradually add the superfine sugar and cream of tartare and continue beating until thick and glossy. Spoon 1 tablespoon lemon curd into the bottom of each pie. Spoon the meringue into a pastry bag with a star tip, then pipe on top of the curd. Bake 12 to 15 minutes until the meringue is just browning on the top. Leave to cool before serving.

Chocolate & Raspberry Tart

PER SERVING:
 FAT 6G (OF WHICH SATURATES 3.8G)
 CALORIES 192
PREPARATION TIME: 20 MINUTES, PLUS MAKING
 THE PASTRY AND 2 HOURS CHILLING
BAKING TIME: 25 MINUTES

Dark chocolate is full of antioxidants so a little bit is considered good for you. And, this indulgent chocolate treat is so easy to make and so delicious it's worth its place in the book.

Heat the oven to 350°F and lightly spray a 9-inch deep, fluted nonstick tart pan with low-calorie cooking oil spray.

Roll out the dough on a lightly floured work surface until ⅛ inch thick. Line the bottom and side of the prepared pan, pushing the dough into the flutes and leaving any overhanging dough. Cover with plastic wrap and chill 10 minutes.

Meanwhile, put the chocolate in a large heatproof bowl and rest it over a saucepan of simmering water, making sure the bottom of the bowl does not touch the water. Heat, stirring, until the chocolate melts. Mix together the cocoa powder, milk and vanilla extract. Fold the mixture into the chocolate with 2 tablespoons boiling water. Leave to cool to blood heat.

Line the dough with parchment paper and cover with baking beans. Bake 12 minutes, then remove the paper and beans. Brush the pastry with egg white, then bake 10 minutes longer, or until golden brown. Remove the pan from the oven and trim off any excess pastry, using a serrated knife.

In a clean bowl, beat the egg whites, using an electric mixer, until stiff peaks form. Gradually add the sugar and continue beating until thick. Fold the crème fraîche into the chocolate. Stir in one-third of the egg whites, then fold in the remainder. Spoon

Makes a 9-inch tart (12 servings)

low-calorie cooking oil spray, for greasing
1 recipe quantity Guilt-free Piecrust Dough
 (see page 18)
a little all-purpose flour, for dusting
1 egg white

FOR THE CHOCOLATE FILLING:
heaped 1 cup dark chocolate chips,
 70% cocoa solids
1 tablespoon unsweetened cocoa powder
2 tablespoons skim milk
2 teaspoons vanilla extract
2 egg whites
2 tablespoons sugar
3½ tablespoons low-fat crème fraîche or sour cream

FOR THE RASPBERRY TOPPING:
3¼ cups raspberries
1 tablespoon confectioners' sugar, sifted

 2 days

into the baked pastry case and smooth the top. Put in the refrigerator 2 hours to set. Put the raspberries on top and sprinkle with confectioners' sugar to serve.

Blueberry & White Chocolate Tart

PER SERVING:
    FAT 5G (OF WHICH SATURATES 2.75G)
    CALORIES 130
PREPARATION TIME: 15 MINUTES, PLUS
    40 MINUTES CHILLING
BAKING TIME: 20 MINUTES

When is comes to lower-fat, lower-calorie recipes, white chocolate is usually a no-go area, but I just love it—for me it's a guilty pleasure, even though I know, as a chef, it is not really chocolate. So I was determined to include it in this book, and the best way to use it if you are watching those all-important numbers is to mix it with something else, like buttermilk, and cut down on the sugar in other areas of the recipe.

Makes a 12-inch tart (12 servings)

FOR THE BLUEBERRY TART:
7 ounces rolled light puff pastry dough
a little all-purpose flour, for dusting
1 egg, beaten
2½ ounces white chocolate, cut into small pieces
4 cups blueberries
7 tablespoons buttermilk

FOR THE WHITE CHOCOLATE TOPPING:
¼ ounce white chocolate, grated
a few mint leaves, torn into pieces

Heat the oven to 400°F and line a cookie sheet with parchment paper.

Unroll the dough on a lightly floured work surface and cut into a 12-inch square. Put the dough on the prepared cookie sheet and mark a ½-inch border around the edges with a knife, making sure you don't cut through the dough. Cover with plastic wrap and chill in the refrigerator 10 minutes.

Brush the border with a little of the beaten egg, taking care not to drip it over the edges, because this would prevent the pastry from rising. Stab the middle of the dough repeatedly with a fork—this is called "docking." Bake 15 minutes, or until golden brown. The border should have risen up and the middle remained flat, creating a rectangular tart case. Transfer the pastry to a wire rack. If the middle has risen up, gently press it back down. To reduce the calories even more, you can remove some pastry layers from the middle. Leave to cool.

While the pastry is cooling, put the white chocolate in a large heatproof bowl and rest it over a pan of simmering water, making sure the bottom of the bowl does not touch the water. Heat, stirring occasionally, until the chocolate begins to melt. Turn

off the heat and leave the chocolate to melt in the residual heat. (This prevents the chocolate from splitting, and white chocolate is prone to split.)

Meanwhile, put ⅔ cup of the blueberries in a skillet with 2 tablespoons water. Bring to a boil, then turn the heat down to low and leave the blueberries to simmer about 4 minutes, or until they start to pop. Puree them, using a hand-blender or by transferring to a blender or food processor, then rub the puree through a strainer.

Once the chocolate melts, gently fold in the buttermilk. Pour the mixture into the tart case and scatter with the remaining blueberries. Chill in the refrigerator 30 minutes, or until set. Just before serving, drizzle the tart with the blueberry sauce, sprinkle with grated chocolate and scatter with the mint leaves.

Perfect Peach Pies

PER SERVING:
   FAT 6G (OF WHICH SATURATES 4G)
   CALORIES 256
PREPARATION TIME: 15 MINUTES
BAKING TIME: 15 MINUTES

Peaches can be so difficult to find perfectly ripe. Cooking with them brings out their natural flavor, so you can use slightly underripe ones for this recipe, although do use the perfectly soft and sweet ones if you can find them. Whichever you use, however, this is a delicious dessert.

Heat the oven to 375°F.

Put the peach halves, cut-side up, in a baking dish. If they do not sit flat, cut a thin slice off the rounded side so they are steady. Put an amaretti cookie in the hole of each peach where the pit once was, then add a splash of the amaretto. (You can leave this out if you are feeding children.)

Work with one half-sheet of phyllo pastry dough at a time, keeping the sheets you are not using covered in a damp dish towel to prevent them from drying out. Brush each sheet of phyllo dough with a little melted butter (they don't have to be completely covered), then scrunch 1 sheet on top of each peach half.

Squeeze the orange juice into the bottom of the dish and add the remaining amaretto. Bake 15 minutes, or until the phyllo pastry is crisp and golden brown and the peaches are soft. Turn upside down onto serving plates and serve with the crème fraîche, if you like.

Makes 12 pies (6 servings)

6 large ripe peaches, halved and pitted
12 amaretti cookies
6 tablespoons amaretto (optional)
6 sheets phyllo pastry dough, each 13½ x 12 inches,
   cut in half
4 tablespoons butter, melted
juice of 1 large orange
¾ cup low-fat crème fraîche, to serve (optional)

Pear & Blackberry Pie

PER SERVING:
   FAT 3G (OF WHICH SATURATES 1.75G)
   CALORIES 115
PREPARATION TIME: 20 MINUTES, PLUS
   30 MINUTES CHILLING
BAKING TIME: 30 MINUTES

My maternal grandmother was the queen of pies. I can generally eat a dish in a restaurant or café and get home and recreate it—that's habit and a skill most chefs pick up. But I just cannot make an apple pie like my grandmother. It's not human nature to admit our shortcomings, but this is mine—I can't do it. So I have given up and I now make other pies instead. This one is my favorite and—although I say so myself—it is blinking good!

To make the dough, put the flour in a large bowl, then rub in the butter, using your fingertips, until the mixture resembles coarse bread crumbs. Stir in the sugar, then use a fork to blend the ricotta into the mix. Add the orange zest, then gradually add about 1 tablespoon water, a drop at a time, and mix to a dough. Add the water very gradually, because all flours absorb different amounts of water. Roll the dough into a ball and flatten, then wrap in plastic wrap and chill in the refrigerator 30 minutes.

While the dough is chilling, peel, core and slice the pears. Put them in a large bowl with the blackberries. Dust with the cornstarch and toss everything together, then drizzle the agave syrup over and mix once more.

Heat the oven to 350°F and line a cookie sheet with parchment paper.

Roll out the dough on a lightly floured work surface into a 12-inch circle and put it on the prepared cookie sheet. Scatter the bottom of the dough with the semolina, which will help absorb any juices and prevent the pie from having a soggy bottom. Pile the fruit in the middle of the dough and bring the

Makes a 10-inch pie (12 servings)

FOR THE RICOTTA PIECRUST DOUGH:
1 cup plus 3 tablespoons all-purpose flour, plus extra
2 tablespoons butter
1 tablespoon sugar
3 tablespoons ricotta cheese
grated zest of 1 orange

FOR THE PEAR & BLACKBERRY FILLING:
4 pears
2 cups blackberries
1 tablespoon cornstarch
1 tablespoon agave syrup
1 tablespoon dried semolina or couscous
1 egg, beaten
1 tablespoon honey
juice of 1 orange

side of the dough up around the fruit. This doesn't have to be neat—you want it rustic. If it does crack, just patch it up. Brush the outside of the dough with a little beaten egg. Bake 30 minutes, or until the fruit is soft, but not mushy, and the pastry is cooked and golden brown. Transfer to a wire rack to cool.

Meanwhile, put the honey and orange juice in a small saucepan and bring to a boil. Turn the heat down to low and simmer about 2 minutes until the mixture is syrupy. Brush this over the baked pie before serving.

Spiced Rhubarb Cobbler

PER SERVING:
  FAT 3.7G (OF WHICH SATURATES 1.9G)
  CALORIES 176
PREPARATION TIME: 20 MINUTES
BAKING TIME: 30 MINUTES

"It will give you tummy ache if you keep eating it like that!" Those were the wise words of my mother as I sat dunking sticks of rhubarb in the sugar bowl. Unfortunately, as all mothers are, she was right. Tummy ache was always the consequence of the strange snacking habits of a six-year-old Gee. I still love the tartness of rhubarb and try not to oversweeten it in desserts, but I have also learned to wait until it is cooked before eating it. When I was working on a TV show many years ago, one of the chefs spiced their rhubarb dish with star anise and cinnamon and, although I can't remember who it was, I am using the idea as the starting point for this recipe, so thank you for the idea whoever you were.

Heat the oven to 350°F.

Beat together the butter and sugar in a large bowl, using an electric mixer, until light and creamy. Mix in the flours, baking powder and cinnamon, then add the egg and three-quarters of the milk and mix to make a thick batter, adding a little more milk. if necessary. You want a thick, sticky batter. You can always add more liquid, but it's a little difficult to take it away!

Put the rhubarb in a 10- x 7-inch oval baking dish and pour the agave syrup over. Scrape the seeds from the vanilla bean into the syrup, then add the vanilla bean, star anise, cinnamon stick, cardamom pods and orange zest.

Put the orange juice in a bowl and blend to a paste with the cornstarch. Add this to the rhubarb, mix everything together, then spread evenly in the dish.

Makes a 10- x 7-inch oval cobbler (12 servings)

FOR THE COBBLER TOPPING:
3 tablespoons butter, soft
⅔ cup sugar
1 cup plus 2½ tablespoons wholewheat flour
¾ cup plus 1 tablespoon self-rising flour,
    plus extra for dusting
1 teaspoon baking powder
1 teaspoon ground cinnamon
1 egg, beaten
½ cup skim milk
¼ cup rolled oats

FOR THE RHUBARB FILLING:
4 cups washed rhubarb chopped
    into ¾-inch pieces
4 tablespoons agave syrup
1 vanilla bean, split in half lengthwise
1 star anise
1 cinnamon stick
2 cardamom pods
grated zest and juice of 1 orange
1 teaspoon cornstarch

Dip two spoons in a little flour, then put spoonfuls of the batter mixture on top of the rhubarb, leaving little gaps in between each spoonful, until you have used all the batter. Scatter the oats over. Bake 30 minutes, or until golden brown. Serve hot.

Apple & Plum Crumble

PER SERVING: 6
   FAT 5.6G (OF WHICH SATURATES 3.5G)
   CALORIES 219
PREPARATION TIME: 20 MINUTES
BAKING TIME: 25 MINUTES

This is a perfect Sunday afternoon dessert after a classic roast. If you have the odd pear, a few blackberries or other bits of fruit that need using up, pop them in as well.

Heat the oven to 350°F. Put the apples and plums in a bowl and mix with the cinnamon, orange zest and juice. Put the fruit into six ⅔-cup ramekins.

Mix together the sugar and flour in a bowl and rub in the butter until the mixture resembles bread crumbs. Finally drizzle the agave syrup over and stir it in. Scatter the crumble mixture over the fruit.

Bake 25 minutes, or until the apples are tender and the top is golden brown. Serve hot.

Makes 6 crumbles (6 servings)

4½ cups peeled and cored dessert apples cut into
   ½-inch chunks
4 plums, pitted and cut into ½-inch chunks
1 teaspoon ground cinnamon
grated zest and juice of 1 orange
2 tablespoons sugar
¾ cup plus 2½ tablespoons self-rising flour
3 tablespoons butter
2 tablespoons agave syrup

   3 months assembled, but unbaked

Meringues & Other Treats

Clouds are fat- and calorie-free, but don't taste nearly as good

That's true—and they are more difficult to make! For many years, meringues were my most feared baked dish, which is never a good thing when you are known for your baking.

When I was a junior working behind the scenes of a TV show in the prep kitchen, fear would pass over me when I saw the word "meringue" on the call sheet. If I was in a bad mood or just really tired after an early alarm for work, my meringue mixture would always look like soup, rather than light, fluffy clouds. It was as if they could judge my mood.

After a particularly bad day in the kitchen when I had made four batches of souplike mixture for a Michelin-starred chef, I arrived home at 10 p.m. and made batch after batch of meringues and baked until 2 a.m. I just needed to get over it—and I did. I can now very happily make meringues, whether I am in a good or bad mood, but I do smile every time they turn out right.

Meringue Nests with Rose Cream & Fresh Berries

PER SERVING:
FAT 1.2G (OF WHICH SATURATES 0.8G)
CALORIES 124
PREPARATION TIME: 15 MINUTES
BAKING TIME: 2 HOURS

I always know when my mom is on a low-fat diet, because there are meringues in the cupboard—they are the perfect, low-fat treat when a sweet craving hits. I've given the classic combination a light, healthy makeover by substituting fat-free yogurt and low-fat crème fraîche or sour cream for the usual heavy cream. The slightly sour taste of the yogurt is balanced by the sweetness of the honey and meringue, and the low-fat crème fraîche adds a touch of creaminess, so there are not any taste sacrifices with this low-fat dessert.

Heat the oven to 225°F and two sheets of parchment paper to fit two cookie sheets. Draw six 3¼-inch circles in pencil on the paper.

In a clean bowl, beat the egg whites, using an electric mixer, until stiff peaks form. Gradually add half the sugar and continue beating until thick and glossy, then use a large metal spoon to gently fold in the rest of the sugar. Put the meringue mixture into a pastry bag fitted with a large star tip. Dab a little of the mixture on the corners of the prepared cookie sheet to hold the parchment paper in place, then put the paper on the cookie sheets so the pencil marks are underneath, but visible through the paper. Pipe the meringue mixture into 6 little nests, using the circles as a guide. Start each with a "blob" in the middle and pipe a spiral around it, then pipe a circle on the outside edge to create a raised border. Repeat to make 6 meringues in total.

Bake the meringue nests 2 hours, or until dry, then transfer to a wire rack to cool.

Makes 6 meringues (6 servings)

4 egg whites
¾ cup plus 1 tablespoon sugar
¾ cup fat-free plain Greek yogurt
3 tablespoons low-fat crème fraîche or sour cream
1 tablespoon honey
a few drops rose water or vanilla extract
2 handfuls mixed berries, such as raspberries, blueberries and sliced strawberries

 7 days before assembling

Mix together the yogurt, crème fraîche, honey and rose water, then spoon some into the middle of each nest. Top with the berries to serve.

Mulled Wine Pavlova

PER SERVING:
FAT 0G
CALORIES 228
PREPARATION TIME: 30 MINUTES
BAKING TIME: 1½ HOURS

This makes a great centerpiece dessert at any time of year, but is especially perfect for Christmas. The deep color of the poached fruits and their spiced aroma makes the house smell like Christmas, and it's a good dessert for sharing.

Heat the oven to 300°F and cut a sheet of parchment paper to fit a cookie sheet. Draw a 9-inch circle on the paper, then put it on the cookie sheet so the pencil marking is underneath but still visible.

In a large, clean bowl, beat the egg whites, using an electric mixer, until stiff peaks form. Gradually add the sugar and continue beating until thick and glossy. Gently fold in the cornstarch and wine vinegar. Spoon the mixture onto the paper, starting with the outside of the circle and then spooning the remaining meringue into the middle to create a crater. Bake 1½ hours, then turn the oven off and leave the pavlova in the oven until completely cool.

Mix together the agave syrup and yogurt. Stir the seeds from the vanilla bean into the yogurt, cover and chill in the refrigerator. (Reserve the bean.)

While the meringue is baking and cooling, put the wine, orange juice, brown sugar, reserved vanilla bean, spices and orange zest in a saucepan and bring to a boil. Add the pears, reduce the heat to low and simmer 5 minutes, or until the pears are starting to soften. Add the plums and simmer 1 minute longer. Remove the pan from the heat and leave the fruit to cool. Transfer 4 tablespoons of the poaching liquid to a small pan and bring to a boil, then simmer until it reduces to a thick syrup. Leave the syrup to cool.

Makes a 9-inch meringue (12 servings)

FOR THE MERINGUE:
4 egg whites
1 cup plus 1 tablespoon superfine sugar
1 teaspoon cornstarch
1 teaspoon white wine vinegar

FOR THE YOGURT FILLING:
1 tablespoon agave syrup
¾ cup plus 2 tablespoons thick, fat-free plain yogurt
1 vanilla bean, split in half lengthwise

FOR THE FRUIT TOPPING:
¾ cup plus 2 tablespoons red wine
¾ cup plus 2 tablespoons orange juice
3¾ tablespoons packed dark soft brown sugar
1 cinnamon stick
1 star anise
5 black peppercorns
grated zest of 1 orange
4 pears, peeled, with stems left on
4 plums, halved and pitted
4 figs, halved

5 days before assembling

When ready to serve, spoon the yogurt into the middle of the pavlova. Remove the fruit from the liquid using a slotted spoon and drain well. (I freeze the remaining liquid for the next time.) Cut the cores out of the pears from underneath so they remain whole. Pile the pears, plums and figs in the middle of the pavlova. Finally drizzle over the reduced poaching liquid and serve.

Mango & Basil Meringue Roulade

PER SERVING:
FAT 1.3G (OF WHICH SATURATES 1.6G)
CALORIES 105
PREPARATION TIME: 30 MINUTES
BAKING TIME: 15 MINUTES

Mango, lime and basil are a classic flavor combination in Thai cooking, albeit Thai basil. The sweetness of the mango is cut perfectly by the lime, while its perfumed flavor is brought out by the basil. Basil has a tendency to turn dark when it gets wet or is cut, so roll everything up at the last minute and the dessert will look its best.

Heat the oven to 350°F and line a 9- x 13-inch jelly-roll pan with parchment paper.

In a large, clean bowl, beat the egg whites, using an electric mixer, until stiff peaks form. You should be able to turn the bowl upside down without the whites falling out. Gradually add the superfine sugar and continue beating until thick and glossy. Spoon the mixture into the prepared pan and spread it out evenly. Bake 15 minutes, or until crisp and light golden. Leave to cool completely in the pan.

While the meringue is cooling, peel the mangoes. Cut the cheeks from both mangoes by cutting straight down each side of the fruit, then leave the flesh to one side. Remove any remaining flesh from the seed and put it in a small food processor along with half the flesh and blend to a puree. Cut the remaining mango flesh into thin slices.

Mix together half the mango puree and all the crème fraîche, the lime zest and a squeeze of the juice. Reserve the remaining puree. Gather the basil leaves together and shred with a knife. Stir these into the crème fraîche and mango mixture.

Put a large piece of parchment paper on a work surface and quickly invert the meringue in its pan onto the paper. Remove the pan and carefully

Makes about a 13-inch roulade (12 servings)

4 egg whites
1 cup less 1 tablespoon superfine sugar
2 large ripe mangos
3 tablespoons low-fat crème fraîche
grated zest and juice of 1 lime
10 basil leaves
1 tablespoon confectioners' sugar, for dusting (optional)

peel back the parchment paper from the bottom. Turn the meringue so the short end is nearest you. Spoon the mango puree and crème fraîche mixture onto the meringue and spread it evenly, leaving a ½-inch border clear at the far end. Put the mango slices horizontally on top of the puree.

Using the parchment paper to help you, roll the meringue up, starting at the short edge nearest to you and continuing to roll everything up until you get to the end, making sure you finish with the edge underneath.

Dust lightly with confectioners' sugar, if you like, then cut into 12 slices and serve with the remaining mango puree.

Apple & Ginger Strudel

Apple strudel is a delicious, fruity and naturally light dessert—but it can easily end up with a soggy bottom. In this recipe, however, the bread crumbs help soak up any juices, so there's a much better chance of a crispy one. If only getting rid of a saggy bottom was that simple!

Heat the oven to 375°F and line two cookie sheets with parchment paper. Mix together the apples, orange zest and juice, preserved ginger, ground ginger, raisins and cornstarch.

Unroll the phyllo pastry dough sheets and put one on the cookie sheet, keeping the sheets you are not using covered in a damp dish towel to prevent them from drying out. Spray with a little low-calorie cooking oil spray, then put the next sheet of dough on top and spray again. Repeat with one more sheet, then do the same process on the other tray, making 2 strudels with 3 sheets of phyllo dough on each. Do not spray the top sheets of dough with oil, but instead sprinkle the bread crumbs over, leaving a ¾-inch border all the way around.

Divide the apple mixture between the 2 top sheets of dough, keeping the border around the edges. Roll the dough up lengthwise, tucking in everything as you go so you have a long cylinder with the seam on the bottom. Spray with a little more oil.

Bake 30 minutes, or until the strudel is golden. Cut into portions and serve hot or cold.

PER SERVING:
 FAT 1.3G (OF WHICH SATURATES 0.5G)
 CALORIES 213
PREPARATION TIME: 35 MINUTES
BAKING TIME: 30 MINUTES

Makes 2 strudels (6 servings)

5½ cups peeled and cored dessert apples, cut
 into ½-inch chunks
grated zest of 1 orange
juice of ½ orange
6 balls preserved ginger, finely diced
1 teaspoon ground ginger
⅓ cup raisins
1 teaspoon cornstarch
6 sheets phyllo pastry dough, 13½ x 12 inches
low-calorie cooking oil spray
4 tablespoons dried bread crumbs

 3 months

Jelly Roll

PER SERVING:
FAT 2.8G (OF WHICH SATURATES 1G)
CALORIES 196
PREPARATION TIME: 30 MINUTES
BAKING TIME: 15 MINUTES

This is a case of jazzing up my jelly roll. Store-bought jelly rolls are usually an ultrasweet sponge, cake filled with vast amounts of super-sweet, cheap jam that has probably never seen a strawberry in its life. This recipe, on the other hand, is filled with fresh fruit and served with a berry compote, making it perfect for a super dessert.

Heat the oven to 400°F and line a 9- x 13-inch jelly roll pan with parchment paper.

Put the eggs and sugar in a large bowl and beat, using an electric mixer, for about 5 minutes until light and creamy. Use a large metal spoon to fold in the flour, taking care not to overmix at this stage. Spoon the mixture into the prepared pan and smooth the surface. Bake 7 to 10 minutes until light golden and springy to the touch.

Put a large piece of parchment paper on a flat surface. Carefully turn the sponge out onto the paper and peel away the lining paper, then cover with a clean dish towel and leave to cool.

Meanwhile, put the frozen mixed berries and agave syrup in a saucepan over medium heat. Scrape the seeds from the vanilla bean into the syrup, then add the vanilla bean and bring to a simmer. Turn the heat down to low and simmer about 5 minutes until the berries start to release their juices. Simmer 5 minutes longer, or until slightly thicker. Leave to cool until ready to use, removing the vanilla bean.

When the cake is cool, spread the yogurt over and scatter with the berries. Position the cake so the short edge is nearest you. Cut off a ½-inch strip from the edge nearest to you, but leave

Makes about a 13-inch roll (6 servings)

3 eggs
⅓ cup sugar
⅔ cup self-rising flour
2 cups frozen mixed berries
3 tablespoons agave syrup
1 vanilla bean, split in half lengthwise
7 tablespoons low-fat strawberry or raspberry yogurt, as natural as possible, flavored and sweetened with fruit
1⅔ cups mixed berries, large ones like strawberries cut in quarters

it in the same place to give you a pivot point to roll the sponge around. Using the parchment paper to help you, roll the cake up, making sure you finish with the seam on the bottom. Cut the jelly roll into 6 slices and serve with the berry sauce.

Passion Fruit Mille-feuille

PER SERVING:
FAT 4.2G (OF WHICH SATURATES 2.5G)
CALORIES 107
PREPARATION TIME: 35 MINUTES
BAKING TIME: 16 MINUTES

Mille-feuille literally translates as "a thousand leaves," which are represented by the layers of puff pastry in the traditional version. For us, however, a thousand leaves is a little excessive, so I have adapted the recipe to use phyllo pastry. You still get thin layers of crisp pastry with a creamy filling between, but with far fewer calories and less fat. This makes a great summer dessert.

Heat the oven to 350°F and spray a nonstick cookie sheet with a little low-calorie cooking oil spray.

Take 2 sheets of phyllo dough and lightly brush with a little of the melted butter. Put another sheet of dough on top of each one, then brush lightly with butter again. Cut each of the piles of dough into 3 long strips, then cut each strip across into 6 squares, so you end up with a total of 36 squares. Cover the prepared cookie sheet with phyllo squares and put another cookie sheet on top. Bake the phyllo squares between the cookie sheets (this stops them from rising) 6 to 8 minutes until golden. Repeat with the remaining dough and leave to cool.

Mix together the ricotta, 2 tablespoons of the confectioners' sugar, the custard and lemon curd. Spoon into a pastry bag fitted with a ½-inch plain tip.

To assemble the mille-feuille, put 12 pastry squares on a board, then pipe a border around the edge of each one using half the filling mixture. Spoon half the passion fruit seeds over, then top each one with another pastry square. Pipe the remaining filling and scatter the passion fruit seeds on top, add a pastry top, then dust with the remaining confectioners' sugar. and serve within an hour or so of assembling.

Makes 12 squares (12 servings)

low-calorie cooking oil spray, for greasing
4 sheets phyllo pastry dough, 13½ x 12 inches
2 tablespoons butter, melted
1 cup plus 2 tablespoons ricotta cheese
3 tablespoons confectioners' sugar, sifted
⅔ cup Guilt-Free Vanilla Custard Sauce (see page 19)
3 tablespoons lemon curd
4 passion fruit, halved and seeds scooped out

Banana & Strawberry Soufflés

PER SERVING:
FAT 2.5G (OF WHICH SATURATES 1.3G)
CALORIES 166
PREPARATION TIME: 20 MINUTES
BAKING TIME: 15 MINUTES

I have a confession to make. Although this recipe is entirely my own, I got the idea from a great chef friend and colleague of mine, Mr. Gino D'Acampo. These are so easy to make, because there isn't the usual custard or roux bottom to make first. Instead the recipe uses pureed bananas and strawberries. So simple, yet effective.

Heat the oven to 400°F. Brush the insides of six ⅔-cup ramekins with melted butter, then dust with 1 tablespoon of the sugar. Put the bananas and strawberries in a blender and blend until smooth.

In a clean bowl, beat the egg whites, using an electric mixer, until stiff peaks form. Gradually add the remaining sugar and continue beating until thick and glossy. Carefully and gradually, fold the egg whites into the banana and strawberry mixture.

Spoon the mixture into the prepared ramekins, leveling the tops with the back of a knife. Run your thumb around the edge of the ramekins so they are clean, then pop them on a baking sheet. Bake 12 to 15 minutes until the soufflés are risen.

Meanwhile, make the sauce. Put the strawberries and sugar in a small saucepan over low heat. Scrape the seeds from the vanilla bean into the mixture, then add the vanilla bean. Heat a few minutes until the strawberries are soft, warmed through and releasing their juices. Remove the pan from the heat, remove the vanilla bean and serve the sauce with the hot soufflés.

Makes 6 soufflés (6 servings)

FOR THE BANANA SOUFFLÉS:
1 tablespon butter, melted
¼ cup sugar, plus 1 tablespoon
   for dusting
3 ripe bananas
1 cup strawberries, hulled
6 egg whites

FOR THE STRAWBERRY SAUCE:
4⅓ cups strawberries, hulled and halved
1 tablespoon sugar
1 vanilla bean, split in half lengthwise

Raspberry & Chocolate Choux Buns

PER SERVING:
    FAT 2G (OF WHICH SATURATES 0G)
    CALORIES 130
PREPARATION TIME: 25 MINUTES, PLUS
    30 MINUTES COOLING
BAKING TIME: 40 MINUTES

For those of you who like profiteroles, this is for you. Instead of being filled with whipped cream, these are packed with fresh raspberries and low-fat chocolate pastry cream. If you want to make the buns in advance, do not fill them, but store the hollow buns in an airtight container for a few days.

Heat the oven to 400°F and line two cookie sheets with parchment paper.

To make the choux pastry dough, put the butter and sugar in a saucepan with ⅔ cup water and bring to a boil over medium heat. Tip in the flour and beat with a wooden spoon 1 minute, or until the mixture is smooth and and comes away from the side of the pan and forms a ball. Take the pan off the heat and gradually beat in enough of the eggs, one at a time, until the mixture is soft enough to drop off the spoon in lumps.

Put 24 teaspoonfuls of the mixture on the prepared cookie sheets, leaving a 1½-inch gap between each. Rinse your hands, then flick a little water over the buns to dampen them. Bake 10 minutes, then turn the heat up to 425°F and bake 15 minutes longer, or until the choux buns are golden brown.

Use a skewer to make a small hole in the bottom of each bun, then turn them upside down (bottoms up) on a wire rack to cool. This lets steam escape and prevents the buns from becoming soggy.

Meanwhile, make the filling. Put the milk and vanilla extract in a saucepan over medium heat until lukewarm. In a separate bowl, mix together the eggs, sugar, cocoa powder and cornstarch, then

Makes 24 buns (12 servings)

3 tablespoons butter
1 teaspoon sugar
½ cup all-purpose flour
2 eggs, beaten
a little confectioners' sugar, for dusting

FOR THE CHOCOLATE & RASPBERRY FILLING:
1½ cups skim milk
1 teaspoon vanilla extract
2 eggs
2 tablespoons sugar
1 tablespoon unsweetened cocoa powder, sifted
⅓ cup cornstarch
2 cups raspberries

 2 days
without filling

 1 month
without filling

gradually beat in the warm milk. Pour the mixture back into a clean pan and put over low heat. Stir continuously until the mixture starts to thicken, beating to get rid of any lumps. Once it starts to bubble, cook 30 seconds, then remove the pan from the heat and spoon into a bowl. Cover the surface with plastic wrap and leave to cool.

When the choux buns and cream are both cool, put the pastry cream into a pastry bag fitted with a ⅝-inch plain tip. Use a serrated knife to slice the buns in half, as if you were slicing a bread roll. Pipe the pastry cream onto the bottom half of each bun, then top with a few raspberries, replace the tops and serve lightly dusted with confectioners' sugar.

Coffee Eclairs

PER SERVING:
 FAT 4.6G (OF WHICH SATURATES 2.5G)
 CALORIES 105
PREPARATION TIME: 25 MINUTES
BAKING TIME: 30 MINUTES

Creamy, soft filling, light, crisp pastry and a splash of frosting—the eclair is the perfect combo. I first made these as an ideal all-in-one dessert for an upscale picnic, because there isn't any need for plates or silverware. The coffee offsets the sweetness to perfection, but you can change the filling to vanilla or chocolate, although chocolate will up the calories slightly.

Heat the oven to 400°F and line a cookie sheet with parchment paper.

Put the butter and sugar in a saucepan with ⅔ cup water and bring to a boil. Turn the heat to low, and beat in the flour with a wooden spoon 1 minute, or until the mixture is smooth and comes away from the side of the pan in a ball. Take off the heat and gradually beat in enough of the eggs until the mix is soft enough to drop off the spoon in lumps.

Spoon the dough into a pastry bag fitted with a ⅝-inch plain tip and pipe 12 lines, 8 x 4 inches, on the paper, leaving a 1-inch gap between each. Rinse your hands and flick a little water them over the dough. Bake 10 minutes, then turn the heat up to 425°F and bake 15 minutes longer, or until the eclairs are golden brown.

Use a skewer to make a small hole in the bottom of each, then turn them upside down (bottoms up) on a wire rack to cool. This lets the steam escape and prevent them from becoming soggy.

Meanwhile, make the filling. Put the milk and coffee in a saucepan over low heat and heat until just lukewarm. Mix together the eggs, sugar and cornstarch, then gradually beat in the milk. Pour the

Makes 12 eclairs (12 servings)

FOR THE ECLAIRS:
3 tablespoons butter
1 teaspoon sugar
⅔ cup all-purpose flour
2 eggs, beaten

FOR THE COFFEE FILLING:
1½ cups skim milk
1 tablespoon instant coffee granules
2 eggs
2 tablespoons sugar
⅓ cup cornstarch

FOR THE CHOCOLATE TOPPING:
1¾ ounces dark chocolate, 70% cocoa solids

  1 month without filling

mixture back into a clean pan over low heat, beating continuously until the mixture starts to bubble and thicken. Cook 30 seconds, then remove from the heat and spoon the pastry cream into a bowl. Cover the surface with plastic wrap and leave to cool.

Put the pastry cream into a pastry bag fitted with a ⅝-inch plain tip. Use a serrated knife to slice the eclairs in half. Pipe a line of cream down the middle of each one and replace the top. Put the chocolate in a large heatproof bowl and rest it over a pan of simmering water, making sure the bottom of the bowl does not touch the water. Heat, stirring, until the chocolate melts. Drizzle the chocolate over the eclairs and leave to set before serving.

Whoopeeeeeeeeee Pies

PER SERVING:
    FAT 1.3G (OF WHICH SATURATES 0.7G)
    CALORIES 115
PREPARATION TIME: 25 MINUTES
BAKING TIME: 10 MINUTES

I know this is an overly excessive use of "e" in a recipe title, but the fact that these are low fat makes people go "whoopeeeeeeeeee," rather than just "whoopee!"

Heat the oven to 325°F and line two baking sheets with parchment paper.

Beat together the sugar and bananas in a bowl until well blended. Mix in the eggs and milk. In a separate bowl, mix together the flour, cocoa powder, baking powder, cream of tartare and salt. Add the wet ingredients to the dry ingredients and mix together well to form a thick batter.

Spoon the batter into a pastry bag fitted with a ⅝-inch plain tip, then pipe 48 circles on the prepared cookie sheets. Alternatively, you can do this by spooning the mixture on with two teaspoons. Bake 8 to 10 minutes until a skewer inserted in the middle comes out clean. Leave the whoopee pies to cool on the baking sheets 5 minutes, then lift off the paper and transfer to a wire rack.

Meanwhile, put the marshmallows in a nonstick saucepan over low heat and gently warm until they melt. Put 1 teaspoon melted marshmallow in the middle of a pie, then top with another and press down lightly. Repeat with the remaining pies and melted marshmallows. Serve warm or leave to cool.

Makes 24 pies (12 servings)

FOR THE WHOOPEE PIES:
¾ cup sugar
2 large ripe bananas, lightly mashed
2 eggs, beaten
1 cup skim milk
2 cups all-purpose flour
1⅓ cups unsweetened cocoa powder, sifted
1½ teaspoons baking powder
½ teaspoons cream of tartare
a pinch fine sea salt

FOR THE MARSHMALLOW FILLING:
2 cups miniature marshmallows

 3 days 3 months without filling

Macaroons

PER SERVING:
  FAT 4G (OF WHICH SATURATES 0.2G)
  CALORIES 200
PREPARATION TIME: 30 MINUTES, PLUS
  15 MINUTES STANDING
BAKING TIME: 15 MINUTES

Macaroons are perennially popular, but be warned —despite being small and light, the buttery, creamy filling can bump up the calories. It's a real case of looks being deceptive. My version is lighter than a normal macaroon, because I have reduced the quantity of ground almonds and used a much lighter filling. They can be tricky to make, but once you have mastered this skill, you can get inventive with flavors and colors, and they never fail to impress. These are best eaten within a couple of days, so store them in an airtight container in the refrigerator—or just tuck in!

Heat the oven to 315°F and line two cookie sheets with parchment paper.

Put the ground almonds and confectioners' sugar in a food processor and blend until really fine. In a clean bowl, beat the egg whites, using an electric mixer, until stiff peaks form. Gradually add the superine sugar and continue beating until thick and glossy. Carefully fold in the almond and confectioners' sugar mixture, using a metal spoon.

If you like, carefully fold in a little pink food coloring and a few drops of almond extract. Spoon the mixture into a pastry bag fitted with a ½-inch round tip. Pipe 48 circles of about 1 inch in diameter onto the cookie sheets. Give the sheets a sharp tap on the countertop, then leave at room temperature 10 to 15 minutes until a skin forms on the surface. Once you can lightly touch the macaroons with your finger and the mixture does not stick to you, they are ready to bake. Bake 15 minutes, or until the macaroons are crisp with dry tops. Transfer to a wire rack to cool.

Makes 24 macaroons (12 servings)

FOR THE MARACOONS:
1 cup very finely ground blanched almonds
1½ cups confectioners' sugar, sifted
3 egg whites
¼ cup plus 1½ tablespoons superfine sugar
a few drops of pink food coloring (optional)
a few drops of almond extract (optional)

FOR THE WHITE CHOCOLATE FILLING:
2½ ounces white chocolate, chopped
7 tablespoons buttermilk
⅔ cup confectioners' sugar, sifted

 3 days

To make the filling, put the chocolate in a large heatproof bowl and rest it over a saucepan of simmering water, making sure the bottom of the bowl does not touch the water. Once the chocolate starts to melt, turn the heat off and let the residual heat melt the rest. This prevents the chocolate from splitting, which white chocolate is particularity prone to do. Once the chocolate melts, stir in the buttermilk, then sift the confectioners' sugar over and stir in. (At this stage you can flavor the filling with peppermint or vanilla extract, if you like.) Leave this mixture to cool and firm up.

Once the macaroons and filling are cool, put the filling in a pastry bag with a ½-inch plain tip. Pipe a little in the middle of half of the macaroons, then top with the remaining macaroons and enjoy.

Golden Raisin Pinwheels

PER SERVING:
FAT 3.5G (OF WHICH SATURATES 1.2G)
CALORIES 285
PREPARATION TIME: 20 MINUTES, PLUS
3 HOURS RISING
BAKING TIME: 20 MINUTES

My mom loves a *pain au raisin* with coffee when she's treating herself, but they are so high in fat from all the butter in the croissant dough that even on a treat day, they seem a little excessive. This is my take on that classic French pastry, replacing croissant dough with traditional bread dough, which is much lighter in calories and fat.

Mix together the flour, salt, sugar, apple pie spice and yeast in a bowl, then make a well in the middle. Gradually add the beaten egg, followed by the milk and mix everything together to make a soft dough.

Turn the dough out onto a lightly floured countertop and knead 10 minutes, or until it is smooth and elastic. Lightly grease a large bowl with low-calorie cooking oil spray. Put the dough in the bowl, cover with plastic wrap and leave in a warm place 2 hours or until it doubles in volume.

Line a cookie sheet with parchment paper. Turn the dough out onto a lightly floured countertop and knock the air out of the dough by punching it with your fist. Use your fingers to press the dough down, then take a rolling pin to roll it into a rectangle that is 8 x 12 x ½ inches. Spread the butter over the surface, then sprinkle the brown sugar, golden raisins and cinnamon over. Roll up tightly, starting at the long edge and tucking everything in as you go, finishing with the seam on top. Pinch the edges together to prevent it from unraveling, then roll it over so the seam is on the bottom.

Using a sharp knife, to cut the long dough roll into 12 pinwheels. Put the pinwheels on their sides on the cookie sheet, so the swirly side faces

Makes 12 pinwheels (12 servings)

4 cups white bread flour, plus extra for dusting
1 teaspoon fine sea salt
3½ tablespoons sugar
2 teaspoons apple pie spice
1 envelop (¼-oz.) rapid-rise yeast
1 egg, beaten
1 cup plus 3 tablespoons skim milk
low-calorie cooking oil spray, for greasing
3 tablespoons butter, soft
2 tablespoons light soft brown sugar
1 cup golden raisins
1 teaspoon ground cinnamon
½ cup confectioners' sugar, sifted

 1 day ❄ 2 months

upward. Cover with a piece of greased parchment paper, then leave to rise 1 hour longer, or until the pinwheels are double in size.

Heat the oven to 400°F. Remove the covering paper and bake the pinwheels 15 to 20 minutes until golden brown, then transfer to a wire rack to cool.

Meanwhile, put the confectioners' sugar in a bowl and add about 2 tablespoons water, a teaspoon at a time, until you have a thick paste that slowly runs off a spoon. Drizzle the icing over the pinwheels, then leave to set 5 minutes before tucking into a delicious pinwheel.

Chocolate, Rum & Raisin Samosas

PER SERVING:
    FAT 6G (OF WHICH SATURATES 3.3G)
    CALORIES 256
PREPARATION TIME: 30 MINUTES, PLUS
    20 MINUTES SOAKING
BAKING TIME: 10 MINUTES

We tend to think of samosas as savory snacks, but in India they also make sweet versions, which inspired me to create these. If you have difficulty folding them into the triangle shapes, you can always just roll them into spring roll shapes instead—just make sure you tuck in the ends.

Put the raisins in a bowl with the rum and leave to soak 20 minutes. Heat the oven to 375°F and line a cookie sheet with parchment paper.

Put the chocolate in a large heatproof bowl and rest it over a saucepan of simmering water, making sure the bottom of the bowl does not touch the water. Heat, stirring occasionally, until the chocolate melts. Remove the pan from the heat and stir in the soaked raisins and rum.

Take 1 strip of phyllo dough, keeping the remaining strips covered with a damp dish towel to prevent them from drying out, and put 1 teaspoon of the chocolate mixture at one end. Take one corner next to the chocolate and fold it over, creating a triangle and covering the chocolate mix. Keep folding the dough over, encasing all the filling, to create a triangular-shaped package, stopping before you make the final fold. Brush the end of the dough with a little melted butter, then fold and press the edges to seal. Put it, seam-side down, on the cookie sheet. Brush the top with butter, then repeat with the remaining dough and filling.

Bake 5 to 10 minutes until the samosas are golden brown. Dust with confectioners' sugar and serve with a scoop of frozen yogurt, if you like.

Makes 12 samosas (12 servings)

1⅓ cups raisins
2 tablespoons dark rum
3½ ounces dark chocolate, 70% cocoa solids
4 sheets phyllo pastry dough, 13½ x 12 inches, each cut into thirds lengthwise
2 tablespoons butter, melted
½ teaspoon confectioners' sugar, sifted, for dusting
12 small scoops of Guilt-free Frozen Vanilla Yogurt (see page 21), to serve (optional)

Cranberry & Cinnamon Hot Cross Buns

PER SERVING:
    FAT 4.2G (OF WHICH SATURATES 1.3G)
    CALORIES 276
PREPARATION TIME: 30 MINUTES, PLUS
    2 HOURS 40 MINUTES RISING
BAKING TIME: 15 MINUTES

Traditionally, hot cross buns are eaten during the Christian celebration of Lent, either warm or toasted, but I think these are far too good just to eat once a year. I love the high shine you get on the top, which is achieved by brushing warm syrup over the hot, just-baked buns. Of course, you can leave off the cross if that doesn't seem right in July.

Mix together the white bread flour and cinnamon in a bowl, then rub in the butter, using your fingertips, until the mixture resembles coarse bread crumbs. Stir in the sugar, orange zest and yeast. Make a well in the middle of the flour and add the beaten egg, followed by the milk. Bring everything together to make a soft dough.

Turn the dough out onto a lightly floured countertop and sprinkle the cranberries over, then knead the dough 10 minutes, or until it is elastic and no longer sticky and the cranberries are incorporated. Lightly spray a clean bowl with low-calorie cooking oil spray, put the dough in the bowl, cover with plastic wrap and leave in a warm place to rise 2 hours, or until it doubles in volume.

Line two cookie sheets with parchment paper. Knock the air out of the dough by punching it with your fist, then divide it into 12 equal pieces and shape them into balls. Put them on the prepared cookie sheets, leaving a gap between each one. Cover the buns lightly with a piece of parchment paper and leave in a warm place 40 minutes longer, or until risen.

Heat the oven to 400°F.

Makes 12 buns (12 servings)

4½ cups white bread flour, plus extra for dusting
2 teaspoons ground cinnamon
3 tablespoons butter
¼ cup plus 2½ tablespoon sugar
grated zest of 1 orange
1 envelope (¼-oz.) rapid rise yeast
1 egg, beaten
1 cup plus 3 tablespoons skim milk
½ cup dried cranberries
low-calorie cooking oil spray, for greasing
2 tablespoons all-purpose flour
1 tablespoon golden syrup or honey

  2 months shaped, but unbaked

Mix together the all-purpose flour with a little cold water to make a paste. Spoon into a small pastry bag, then pipe a cross on the top of each bun. Bake 10 to 15 minutes until golden brown and risen. Transfer to a wire rack to cool slightly.

Warm the golden syrup in a saucepan or the microwave and brush over the hot tops to give them a nice glaze. Serve warm or toasted.

Scones

PER SERVING:
FAT 3.2G (OF WHICH SATURATES 2.3G)
CALORIES 99
PREPARATION TIME: 15 MINUTES
BAKING TIME: 15 MINUTES

We would always telephone Nanny (my mom's mom) before setting off on the hour-long drive to her house to let her know we were on our way. By the time we arrived, the kitchen would be filled with fruit scones for Mom and Dad, cheese ones for my sister and plain ones for me. They would literally cover every surface. We would all take doggy bags home to pop in the freezer. That's why this recipe reminds me of Nanny and her amazing scones.

Heat the oven to 400°F and lightly flour a nonstick cookie sheet.

Put the flour in a large bowl, then rub in the butter, using your fingertips, until the mixture resembles bread crumbs. Stir in the sugar, then use a fork to gradually mix in the milk and mix to a soft dough.

Turn the dough out onto a lightly floured countertop and knead very lightly until smooth. (Kneading it too much will develop the gluten in the flour and make the scones tough.) Roll the dough out until it is ¾ inch thick, then cut out the scones using a 2-inch round biscuit cutter. Gather together any off-cuts and carefully knead lightly again, then reroll and cut out any remaining scones.

Put the scones on the prepared cookie sheet and brush the tops with a little milk. Bake 12 to 15 minutes until risen and golden brown.

Transfer to a wire rack to cool. Put a clean dish towel over the cooling scones 5 minutes, then remove the towel and leave to cool completely. This just helps put some steam back into the scones so they are extra light in the middle.

Makes 12 scones (12 servings)

1¾ cups plus 1 tablespoon self-rising flour,
    plus extra for dusting
3 tablespoons butter
2 tablespoons sugar
⅔ cup skim milk, plus 1 tablespoon, for glazing

 1 day 3 months

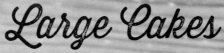

Large Cakes

Love at first bite

Big cakes are the kings and queens of the dessert table. They look so impressive placed on beautiful cake stands and plates and are perfect to serve for celebrations with friends and family. They are the cakes for sharing.

Big cakes are often great ones to start making if you are a novice baker, because their size means they look impressive, even if they are not frosted perfectly. There is also rarely any need for technical piping or precise division of batter between cupcake cases.

One problem that occurs with big cakes, however, which often does not affect smaller, individual cakes, is that the baking time can vary, depending on your oven. If you find the cakes are browning too quickly, before they are baked through, cover the top of the cake with a piece of kitchen foil until it finishes baking. Next time, reduce the oven temperature by 50°F and everything should be fine.

Happy baking and very happy celebrating.

Apple & Cinnamon Crumble Cake

PER SERVING:
FAT 3.4G (OF WHICH SATURATES 1.5G)
CALORIES 182
PREPARATION TIME: 15 MINUTES
BAKING TIME: 1 HOUR

When a combination works as well as apple and cinnamon, why only use it in a traditional crumble? This recipe covers the best of both worlds: a delicious cake made with low-fat yogurt is combined with chunks of apple, keeping it moist in the middle, and then complemented by a crumbly cinnamon topping for a bit of extra crunch. The slices are also great toasted.

Heat the oven to 350°F. Grease a 9½- x 5½-inch bread pan with low-calorie cooking oil spray.

Beat together the eggs, ½ cup sugar, yogurt and vanilla extract, using an electric mixer, until light and creamy. Sift the self-rising flour, 1 teaspoon of the cinnamon and the baking powder over, then stir in the grated and diced apples. Spoon the batter into the prepared bread pan.

Put the all-purpose flour in a large bowl, then rub in the butter, using your fingertips, until the mixture resembles fine bread crumbs. Stir in the remaining cinnamon and 1 tablespoon sugar, then sprinkle the mixture over the top of the cake. Bake 1 hour, or until the top is golden brown and a skewer inserted in the middle comes out clean.

Leave the cake to cool in the pan 10 minutes, then carefully transfer to a wire rack to cool completely.

Makes a 9½- x 5½-inch loaf (12 servings)

low-calorie cooking oil spray, for greasing
3 eggs
½ cup plus 2 tablespoons sugar, plus an extra 2 tablespoons for the crumble topping
¾ cup plus 2 tablespoons fat-free plain yogurt
1 teaspoon vanilla extract
1¾ cups plus 1 tablespoon self-rising flour
2 teaspoons ground cinnamon
2 teaspoons baking powder
3 apples, cored, skin on, 2 grated and 1 chopped into ½-inch dice
⅓ cup all-purpose flour
2 tablespoons butter

 2 days   ❄ 3 months

Austrian-style Rhubarb Cake

PER SERVING:
FAT 4.4G (OF WHICH SATURATES 0.2G)
CALORIES 154
PREPARATION TIME: 15 MINUTES PLUS
30 MINUTES MARINATING
BAKING TIME: 40 MINUTES

My dear school friend Heidi's mother is from Austria and can I can remember going around to Heidi's house and being fed cakes and baked goods that tasted like nothing I had ever eaten. I was absolutely fascinated by them all, but three stood out for me—Christmas cookies, apricot dumplings and this rhubarb cake. This is my adaptation of her cake, just a little lighter.

Heat the oven to 350°F. Grease a 9-inch loose-bottomed cake pan with low-calorie spray oil and line the bottom with parchment paper.

Put the chunks of rhubarb in a bowl and sprinkle 2 tablespoons of the sugar over. Leave 30 minutes, then drain off any water and pat the rhubarb cubes dry. Dust with cornstarch and toss together.

Beat together the butter and sugar, using an electric mixer, until light and creamy. Beat in the eggs, one at a time, then sift the flour and baking powder over and fold them in.

Spoon the batter into the prepared cake pan and smooth the top a little with a spatula. Top this with the rhubarb. Bake 40 minutes, or until a skewer inserted in the middle comes out clean.

Leave the cake to cool in the pan 15 minutes, then transfer to a wire rack to cool completely.

Makes a 9-inch cake (12 servings)

low-calorie cooking oil spray, for greasing
hcaped 4 cups trimmed and chopped rhubarb
½ cup plus 2 tablespoons sugar
1 tablespoon cornstarch
3 tablespoons butter, soft
2 eggs
1⅓ cups plus 1 tablespoon all-purpose flour
2 teaspoons baking powder

Raspberry, Pear & Oat Loaf

PER SERVING:
  FAT 5G (OF WHICH SATURATES 2.5G)
  CALORIES 177KCAL
PREPARATION TIME: 15 MINUTES, PLUS
  15 MINUTES SOAKING
BAKING TIME: 1 HOUR

I believe oats are a super food—they soak up cholesterol in your blood, helping to reduce it naturally. I designed this cake for my dad, who has high cholesterol, despite following a healthy lifestyle. This is a treat for him, because it combines his favorite fruit, pears, with oats that hold moisture in the cake and make it utterly delicious and almost positively good for him—and you, too

Put the oats in a large bowl. Bring the apple juice to a boil in a small saucepan, then pour it over the oats and leave them to soak 15 minutes.

Meanhile, heat the oven to 350°F. Lightly grease a 9½- x 5½-inch bread pan with low-calorie cooking oil spray.

Beat together the butter, sugar and vanilla extract, using an electric mixer, until light and creamy. Beat in the eggs one at a time. Fold in the flour and baking powder, then fold this mixture into the soaked oats. Finally, stir in the raspberries and diced pears.

Spoon the batter into the prepared bread pan and sprinkle with remaining 1 tablespoon oats. Bake 1 hour, or until golden brown and a skewer inserted in the middle comes out clean. Turn out and transfer to a wire rack to cool.

Makes a 9½- x 5½-inch loaf (12 servings)

heaped 1 cup rolled oats, plus 1 tablespoon
  for sprinkling
⅔ cup apple juice
low-calorie cooking oil spray, for greasing
3 tablespoons butter, soft
¼ cup plus 1½ tablespoons sugar
1 teaspoon vanilla extract
2 eggs
1½ cups self-rising flour
1 teaspoon baking powder
1¼ cups raspberries
2 ripe pears, peeled, cored and cut into ½-inch dice

 2 days   3 months

Orange, Polenta & Thyme Cake

PER SERVING:
FAT 6G (OF WHICH SATURATES 1G)
CALORIES 215
PREPARATION TIME: 25 MINUTES, PLUS
20 MINUTES SOAKING
BAKING TIME: 40 MINUTES

This polenta cake has a totally different texture from a normal sponge cake. There is a slight crunch to it, because the polenta holds its texture when baked. It also absorbs the flavor of the orange as it soaks up the juice and syrup at the end. It's a beautiful summery cake that also makes a contemporary dessert when served warm with low-fat crème fraîche or low-fat sour cream.

Put the polenta in a bowl, pour one-third of the orange juice over and leave to soak about 20 minutes, stirring occasionally. Heat the oven to 325°F and line the bottom of a 9-inch nonstick springform cake pan with parchment paper.

Meanwhile, grate the zest from the oranges and leave to one side. Cut the top and bottom off both oranges and use a small knife to carefully cut off the peel and pith, then slice the oranges into ⅛-inch slices. Arrange these over the bottom of the cake pan and add the thyme sprigs.

Beat together the eggs and sugar, using an electric mixer, until light and creamy, then beat in the oil, the reserved orange zest, the yogurt and thyme leaves. Stir in the soaked polenta.

In a separate bowl, mix together the ground almonds, flour and baking powder. Carefully fold the dry ingredients into the wet ingredients until just combined, then pour the batter into the prepared cake pan and smooth the top a little. Bake 30 to 40 minutes until a skewer inserted in the middle comes out clean.

Makes a 9-inch cake (12 servings)

⅔ cup fine polenta or yellow cornmeal
1¼ cups fresh orange juice
2 oranges
3 thyme sprigs
3 eggs
¾ cup sugar
3 tablespoons olive oil
7 tablespoons fat-free plain yogurt
1 teaspoon thyme leaves
⅓ cup very finely ground blanched almonds
1 cup plus 3 tablespoons all-purpose flour
1 teaspoon baking powder

 2 days ❄ 3 months

While the cake is baking, pour the remaining orange juice into a small saucepan and bring to the boil over high heat. Turn the heat down to low and simmer about 10 minutes until it is thick and syrupy.

Leave the cake to cool completely in the pan, then run a knife around the edge to release the cake. Put a plate on top of the cake and carefully invert it, then remove the pan. Loosen the cake bottom and peel back the paper. Pour the orange juice syrup over the cake and leave to soak in before serving.

Banana & Rum Cake

PER SERVING:
  FAT 3.5G (OF WHICH SATURATES 0.5G)
  CALORIES 279
PREPARATION TIME: 15 MINUTES
BAKING TIME: 30 MINUTES, PLUS MAKING
  THE APPLE PUREE

There are a few things that make my teeth go
a little funny when I have to touch them—you know,
like fingers scratching down a chalkboard. I have
learned to cope with that, but polystyrene and
overripe bananas still freak me out. However, I also
hate wasting food, so I just have to get on with
it when it comes to ripe bananas. (I find grimacing
when peeling helps.) This cake is a perfect way
to use up bananas that are really ripe and soft, and
not just because the hint of rum adds an adult twist
to the proceedings. It tastes just as good made
with honey if you are sharing it with children.

Heat the oven to 350°F and lightly grease an 8-inch
square cake pan with low-calorie cooking oil spray.

Put the eggs, sugar, milk, oil and vanilla extract
in a bowl and beat 5 minutes, using an electric
mixer, until light and creamy, then beat in the apple
puree. Mash the very ripe bananas, then beat them
into the mixture. Sift the flour, baking powder,
baking soda and salt over. Fold everything together
until blended, then spoon the batter into the
prepared pan and smooth the top a little.

Cut the ripe banana into very thin slices on the
diagonal, then arrange the slices on top of the cake.
Bake about 30 minutes until the cake is golden
brown, or a skewer inserted in the middle comes
out clean.

Gently warm the rum and honey in a small
saucepan. Remove the cake from the oven and
brush the rum mixture over the cake. Leave the
cake to cool in the pan 5 minutes, then transfer
to a wire rack to cool completely.

Makes an 8-inch square cake (12 servings)

low-calorie cooking oil spray, for greasing
2 eggs
¾ cup sugar
5 tablespoons skim milk
1 tablespoon sunflower oil
1 tablespoon vanilla extract
4 tablespoons Apple Puree (see page 15)
2 very ripe bananas, and 1 ripe banana
1¾ cups plus 1 tablespoon all-purpose flour
1 tablespoon baking powder
1 teaspoon baking soda
½ teaspoon fine sea salt
2 tablespoons rum
2 teaspoons honey

 3 days 3 months

Lemon, Rosemary & Poppy Seed Cake

PER SERVING:
  FAT 5.3G (OF WHICH SATURATES 2.6G)
  CALORIES 250KCAL
PREPARATION TIME: 10 MINUTES, PLUS AT LEAST
  15 MINUTES SOAKING
BAKING TIME: 30 MINUTES

Cakes and herbs might not seem to be natural bedfellows, but herbs can make familiar cakes, such as lemon and poppy seed, into totally new creations. Lemon and rosemary work perfectly together in savory dishes and marinades and now they can lie side by side in sweet treats, too.

Put the poppy seeds in a bowl, pour the warm milk over and leave to soak at least 15 minutes. Heat the oven to 350°F and grease a 10-inch Bundt pan or fluted ring mold with a little low-calorie cooking oil spray.

Beat together the butter and sugar, using an electric mixer, until light and creamy. Add the eggs, flour, soaked poppy seeds, lemon zest, yogurt and chopped rosemary and mix together well.

Spoon the batter into the prepared pan and smooth the top a little. Bake 25 to 30 minutes until a skewer inserted in the middle comes out clean. Leave the cake to cool in the pan 5 minutes, then transfer to a wire rack to cool completely.

Once the cake is cool, sift the confectioners' sugar into a small bowl. Beat in the lemon juice, a few drops at a time, mixing to make a paste. Spoon the icing over the top of the cake. Brush the rosemary sprigs with the beaten egg white, using a pastry brush. Sprinkle the superfine sugar over to give them a frosted effect, then put the sprigs of rosemary on the iced cake to serve.

Makes a 10-inch cake (12 servings)

FOR THE LEMON, ROSEMARY & POPPY SEED CAKE:
low-calorie cooking oil spray, for greasing
2 tablespoons poppy seeds
2 tablespoons warm skim milk
3 tablespoons butter, soft
1 cup sugar
3 eggs
2¼ cups plus 2½ tablespoons self-rising flour
grated zest of 2 lemons
7 tablespoons fat-free plain yogurt
1 tablespoon chopped rosemary needles

FOR THE LEMON & ROSEMARY TOPPING:
1 cup confectioners' sugar, sifted
2½ teaspoons lemon juice
3 rosemary sprigs
1 egg white, lightly beaten
1 tablespoon superfine sugar

 3 days

Pear, Cocoa & Walnut Upside-down Cake

PER SERVING:
    FAT 5.6G (OF WHICH SATURATES 0.5G)
    CALORIES 193
PREPARATION TIME: 20 MINUTES
BAKING TIME: 40 MINUTES

As a child, I was fortunate to grow up in a house with a few fruit trees in the backyard. They never fruited gradually, however—all the fruit came at once at the end of September. We had to come up with a variety of recipes other than stewed apples and pears to use up the crop in inventive ways. This upside-down cake was one of my favorites. We always had one or two in the freezer months after the leaves had fallen from the trees. I've made this with fresh pears, but you can use a can of pear halves in natural juice, drained, then you don't need to poach them.

Heat the oven to 350°F and grease the bottom and side of a 9-inch cake pan with low-calorie cooking oil spray.

Put the pears in a saucepan with 2 cups water and the sugar and bring to a boil, then turn the heat down to low and simmer 5 minutes, or until just they are tender when pierced with the tip of a knife. Remove the pears from the heat, drain and leave to cool slightly.

Arrange two-thirds of the pear pieces, cut-sides down, in the bottom of the prepared cake pan, then scatter with the walnut halves. Mix together the brown sugar and cocoa powder, then sprinkle them over the pears. Puree the remaining pear halves and measure out ½ cup of the puree.

To make the topping, mix together the flour, baking powder, cinnamon and cocoa powder in a large bowl. In a separate bowl, beat together the sugar, eggs, pear puree and oil until blended. Add the wet ingredients to the dry ingredients and mix until just combined. Pour the cake batter over the pears

Makes a 9-inch cake (12 servings)

FOR THE WALNUT & CHOCOLATE BOTTOM:
low-calorie cooking oil spray, for greasing
4 pears, peeled, cored and halved or quartered
½ cup sugar
12 walnut halves
1 tablespoon light soft brown sugar
1 tablespoon unsweetened cocoa powder, sifted

FOR THE CHOCOLATE TOPPING:
1 cup plus 3 tablespoons self-rising flour
2 teaspoons baking powder
2 teaspoons ground cinnamon
6 tablespoons unsweetened cocoa powder, sifted
⅔ cup packed light soft brown sugar
2 eggs
3 tablespoons sunflower oil
½ teaspoon confectioners' sugar, sifted, for dusting

 2 days   3 months

in the bottom of the prepared pan and smooth the top a little. Bake about 30 minutes until a skewer inserted in the middle comes out clean. Turn the cake out upside down onto a serving plate, dust with confectioners' sugar and serve warm, or leave to cool completely.

Summer Berry Gateau

PER SERVING:
FAT 5G (OF WHICH SATURATES 2G)
CALORIES 219
PREPARATION TIME: 20 MINUTES, PLUS
20 MINUTES BEATING
BAKING TIME: 35 MINUTES

The word "gateau" conjures up images of decadent cakes filled with whipped cream and berries, and although they look beautiful, I think they can be a little bit sickly sweet and heavy. This cake, on the other hand, is a classic Genoise sponge cake made with very little butter and lots of eggs. Because you beat the eggs for so long, they act as the raising agent and make the sponge super light. And, instead of mountains of whipped cream between the layers, the honey-sweetened yogurt provides a creamy backdrop on which to load the berries.

Makes an 8-inch cake (12 servings)

low-calorie cooking oil spray, for greasing
3¾ tablespoons superfine sugar
6 eggs
3 tablespoons butter
2 cups all-purpose flour
2 tablespoons low-sugar strawberry jam
scant 2 cups fat-free plain Greek yogurt
1 tablespoon honey
2½ cups mixed summer berries

Heat the oven to 350°F. Line the bottoms of two 8-inch round cake pans with parchment paper and grease the sides with a little low-calorie cooking oil spray.

Put the sugar and eggs in a large, heatproof bowl set over a saucepan of simmering water. Turn the heat down to low and beat 15 to 20 minutes, using an electric mixer, until really light and fluffy and doubled in volume. You should be able to drip a "W" shape from the beaters, that will remain on the surface 8 seconds.

Put the butter in a small saucepan over a low heat and when it is foaming, slowly beat it into the egg mixture a drop at a time, beating continuously. Gently fold in the flour, taking care not to overmix. Divide the batter between the prepared pans and smooth the tops a little. Bake 25 minutes, or until a skewer inserted in the middle of each cake comes out clean.

Turn the cakes out onto wire racks to cool. Once they are cool, use a long, serrated knife to cut each cake in half horizontally, giving you 4 layers. Spread one side of each layer with the jam. Mix together the yogurt and honey. Divide the yogurt among the 4 layers, spreading it out over the jam. Layer the cakes on top of each other, then load the top tier with fresh summer berries.

Lemon & Tofu Cheesecake

PER SERVING:
FAT 5.9G (OF WHICH SATURATES 2.4G)
CALORIES 201
PREPARATION TIME: 30 MINUTES, PLUS
1 HOUR CHILLING
BAKING TIME: 55 MINUTES

Replacing some of the cream cheese with super low-fat tofu creates a perfect low-fat cheesecake. Silken tofu has a similar texture to cream cheese and the strong flavor of lemon in the recipe means you will never notice the difference.

Spray a 9-inch deep, loose-bottomed cake pan with a little low-calorie cooking oil spray. Break the crackers into a food processor and blend until fine crumbs form. Melt the butter and agave syrup over low heat, then pour into the crumbs and blend again. Press the cracker crumbs into the bottom of the prepared pan. Chill 1 hour until set.

Heat the oven to 315°F.

To make the cheesecake, put the cream cheese in a food processor and blend until creamy, then add the agave syrup and butter and blend again. Add the tofu and blend once more, then add the eggs one at a time through the funnel and blend well between each addition. Finally, add the milk, lemon zest and juice and cornstarch. Blend everything together, then pour over the crumb crust and smooth the top a little. Bake 45 minutes, or until just set with a very slight wobble in the middle, Turn the oven off and open the door. Leave the cheesecake to cool in the oven until the oven is cold, then cover the cheesecake with a clean dish towel, making sure it does not touch the surface. Transfer to the refrigerator to chill.

Warm the raspberries in a small saucepan with the sugar and 1 tablespoon water until they start to release their juices, then leave to cool. Serve slices of the cheesecake with the cool raspberries.

Makes a 9-inch cake (12 servings)

FOR THE GRAHAM CRACKER CRUST:
low-calorie cooking oil spray, for greasing
2 tablespoons butter
2 tablespoons agave syrup
5 ounces low-fat Graham crackers (about 10)

FOR THE LEMON & TOFU FILLING:
¾ cup plus 2 tablespoons light cream cheese
3 tablespoons agave syrup
2 tablespoons butter, soft
9 ounces silken tofu, drained
2 eggs
3½ tablespoons skim milk
grated zest and juice of 2 lemons
2 tablespoons cornstarch

TO SERVE:
3¼ cups raspberries
1 tablespoon sugar

 3 days 3 months

Carrot & Zucchini Cake

PER SERVING:
FAT 5.5G (OF WHICH SATURATES 1G)
CALORIES 189KCAL
PREPARATION TIME: 15 MINUTES
BAKING TIME: 30 MINUTES

Everybody loves carrot cake, because it is super moist and the natural sweetness of the carrots is highlighted by the spices. The addition of zucchini to this recipe means you can lower the fat content even more, because zucchini add extra moisture, but without losing the carrot flavor. To my gorgeous niece Orlaith, this is known as my Peter Rabbit's Cake. It is a great recipe for children, especially those who are a bit reluctant to eat their veggies, as it counts toward their recommended amount without them even noticing.

Heat the oven to 350°F and line an 8-inch square cake pan with parchment paper.

Put the brown sugar, eggs and oil in a large bowl and beat together 3 minutes, using an electric mixer, to amalgamate and incorporate as much air as possible. Sift the flour, baking soda and spices over and fold them in, mixing well. Stir in the grated carrots and zucchini.

Spoon the batter into the prepared cake pan and smooth the top a little. Bake in the middle of the oven 25 to 30 minutes until a skewer inserted in the middle comes out clean.

Remove the cake from the oven, cover it with a dish towel and leave to cool in the pan 10 minutes, then transfer to a wire rack. Cover once again with the towel and leave to cool completely.

Mix together the cream cheese and sugar. Spread the frosting over the cool cake and sprinkle with the chopped walnuts. Cut into 12 pieces to serve.

Makes an 8-inch square cake (12 servings)

FOR THE CARROT & ZUCCHINI CAKE:
⅔ cup packed dark soft brown sugar
2 eggs
3 tablespoons sunflower oil
1⅔ cups all-purpose flour
1 teaspoon baking soda
heaped 1 teaspoon apple pie spice
½ teaspoon ground ginger
2 teaspoons ground cinnamon
scant 1½ cups peeled and grated carrots
⅔ cup grated zucchini

FOR THE CREAM CHEESE FROSTING:
7 ounces light cream cheese
2 tablespoons sugar
4 walnuts, chopped

 3 days   3 months without topping

Devilishly Good Chocolate Mayonnaise Cake

PER SERVING:
FAT 3.9G (OF WHICH SATURATES 2G)
CALORIES 248
PREPARATION TIME: 25 MINUTES
BAKING TIME: 30 MINUTES

This recipe originally came from my mom. She recorded a similar recipe from a children's TV program my sister was watching many years ago when we still recorded on VHS. My sister clearly remembers playing the video in the living room at a later date and running back and forth to the kitchen with the next instruction, only to then have to rewind it and play it back again. It does beg the question why did they not just watch it, write it down and then bake it. Thank goodness for internet print-outs now. I've adapted the recipe, but the principle remains the same and uses mayonnaise in the ingredients. If you think about it, mayonnaise is simply egg yolks, oil and a dash of vinegar beaten together, and you always add eggs and a fat to a cake—either butter or oil. The only difference is that if you add mayonnaise, these two ingredients are already beaten together, with the added bonus that the vinegar reacts with baking powder to help the cake rise.

Heat the oven to 350°F. Line the bottoms of two 8-inch round cake pans with parchment paper and grease the sides with a little low-calorie cooking oil spray.

Mix together the flour, baking powder, cocoa powder and sugar in a large bowl. Tip the mayonnaise into the bowl, but do not mix anything at this stage—however tempting that might be. Measure 7 ounces boiling water in a measuring jug, then pour the water into the flour bowl and mix everything together thoroughly. Carefully pour the batter into the prepared cake pans. Bake 15 to 25 minutes until a skewer inserted in the middle comes out clean. Transfer to a wire rack to cool completely.

Makes an 8-inch cake (12 servings)

FOR THE CHOCOLATE CAKE:
low-calorie cooking oil spray, for greasing
2¼ cups plus 2½ tablespoon self-rising flour
1½ teaspoons baking powder
4 tablespoons unsweetened cocoa powder, sifted
¾ cup plus 2 tablespoons sugar
¾ cup plus 2 tablespoons light mayonnaise
a few pink rose petals, to decorate

FOR THE CHOCOLATE FROSTING:
2 tablespooons butter
4 tablespoons low-fat evaporated milk
4 tablespoons unsweetened cocoa powder, sifted
1½ cups confectioners' sugar, sifted

 2 days 3 months

When the cake is cool, make the frosting. Put the butter and evaporated milk in a small saucepan over low heat until the butter melts. Put the cocoa powder and confectioners' sugar into the saucepan and mix everything together well. Remove the pan from the heat and cover the surface of the frosting with plastic wrap, then leave to cool 10 minutes until it is not so runny. (The plastic wrap on the surface stops it from forming a skin.)

Pour the cool frosting on top of the cake. Use a metal spatula to spread it toward the edge of the cake and let it run down the side. Smooth the frosting over the whole cake and either leave it with a smooth finish or add strokes of texture. Scatter the rose petals over the top to finish.

Chocolate Cloud Cake

PER SERVING:
    FAT 5.6G (OF WHICH SATURATES 2.5G)
    CALORIES 117
PREPARATION TIME: 10 MINUTES, PLUS
    15 MINUTES BEATING AND CHILLING
    OVERNIGHT
BAKING TIME: 25 MINUTES

This cake is super rich, so you can get a chocolate fix without overeating. This is the dessert I often choose when I have friends come for dinner who are gluten-intolerant. Everybody can enjoy the same dessert and no-one has to miss out—plus it's every chocoholic's dream.

Heat the oven to 350°F. Spray a 9-inch round springform cake pan with low-calorie cooking oil spray and line the bottom with parchment paper.

Bring 5 tablespoons water to a boil in a small saucepan. Add the cocoa powder and instant coffee and stir until smooth. Add the chocolate and vanilla extract and stir again until smooth.

Put the eggs, egg whites and superfine sugar in a heatproof bowl and rest it over a pan of simmering water. Beat about 5 minutes, using an electric mixer, until thick and doubled in volume. Remove the pan from the heat and continue beating 15 minutes until the mixture trails off the beat in ribbons. You should be able to drip a "W" shape from the beaters, which should remain on the surface 8 seconds.

Stir one-third of the egg mixture into the chocolate, then fold in the remainder. Spoon the batter into the prepared pan. Bake 25 minutes, or until the cake is almost set with just a slight wobble in the middle.

Transfer the cake to a wire rack and leave to cool in the pan until it reaches room temperature, then chill 8 hours or overnight.

Makes a 9-inch cake (12 servings)

low-calorie cooking oil spray, for greasing
⅓ cup unsweetened cocoa powder, sifted, plus
    1 teaspoon for dusting
2 teaspoons instant coffee
4½ ounces dark chocolate, 70% cocoa solids,
    finely chopped
½ teaspoon vanilla extract
3 eggs
3 egg whites
¼ cup superfine sugar
1 teaspoon confectioners' sugar, sifted, for dusting

 3 days   3 months without topping

Mix the confectioners' sugar with the remaining cocoa powder, then sprinkle it over the cake to serve.

Earl Grey Quick Bread with Lemon & Passion Fruit

PER SERVING:
  FAT 4.2G (OF WHICH SATURATES 0.4G)
  CALORIES 213
PREPARATION TIME: 20 MINUTES
BAKING TIME: 30 MINUTES

Earl Grey tea is full of the heady aroma of bergamot. Its distinct taste and smell comes from the oil extracted from the zest of the bergamot orange, so it has a citrusy note that is perfect in this delicious cake with its lemony icing.

Heat the oven to 350°F. Line the bottom of a 9-inch round loose-bottomed cake pan with parchment paper and spray the side with a little low-calorie cooking oil spray.

Grind the tea leaves in a mortar and pestle until you have a fine powder. Sift the tea, flour and baking powder into a bowl. Beat together the oil, sugar, eggs and pear puree, using an electric mixer, in a separate bowl. Pour this into the flour mixture and mix well.

Spoon the batter into the prepared cake pan and smooth the top. Bake 30 minutes, or until a skewer inserted in the middle comes out clean. Transfer the cake to a wire rack to cool completely.

Meanwhile, put the confectioners' sugar in a bowl and gradually mix in enough of the lemon juice, a drop at a time, to make a thick paste that will dribble slowly down the side of the cake. Drizzle the cake with the icing, then scatter with the passion fruit seeds to serve.

Makes a 9-inch cake (12 servings)

FOR THE EARL GREY QUICK BREAD:
low-calorie cooking oil spray, for greasing
1½ tablespoons loose-leaf Earl Grey tea (or you can simply empty 3 teabags)
2 cups self-rising flour
2 teaspoons baking powder
3 tablespoons sunflower oil
¾ cup sugar
2 eggs
5 ounces canned pears in natural juice, drained and pureed

FOR THE ICING:
1¼ cups confectioners' sugar, sifted
1 to 2 tablespoons lemon juice
1 passion fruit, halved and seeds scraped out

 3 days

Index

Acknowledgements

I just want to thank a few people for helping me get to this point—you baking from this book. My sister Joss, who helped out no end when it came to doing the admin things for me—without her I would have never made the deadline. Also Grace, who gave me the opportunity in the first place—it takes a leap of faith when taking on a new writer. Wendy, Grace and Jon for being so patient when I lost everything on my computer after it decided to crash. And, finally, Mom and Dad, who let me trash their kitchen as a child when I decided baking was the best form of entertainment—THANK YOU.

NOURISH
EAT WELL, LIVE WELL

We hope you've enjoyed this Nourish book. Here at Nourish we're all about wellbeing through food and drink —irresistible dishes with a serious good-for-you factor. If you want to eat and drink delicious things that set you up for the day, suit any special diets, keep you healthy and make the most of what you can afford, we've got some great ideas to share with you. Come over to our blog for wholesome recipes and fresh inspiration—nourishbooks.com.